How Does Societal Transformation Happen?

Values Development, Collective Wisdom, and Decision Making for the Common Good

Quaker Institute for the Future Pamphlet Series

Quaker Institute for the Future Pamphlets aim to provide critical information and understanding born of careful discernment on social, economic, and ecological realities, inspired by the testimonies and values of the Religious Society of Friends (Quakers). We live in a time when social and ecological issues are converging toward catastrophic breakdown. Human adaptation to social, economic and planetary realities must be re-thought and re-designed. *Quaker Institute for the Future Pamphlets* are dedicated to this calling based on a spiritual and ethical commitment to "right relationship" with Earth's whole commonwealth of life.

Quaker Institute for the Future
<quakerinstitute.org>

How Does Societal Transformation Happen?

Values Development, Collective Wisdom, and Decision Making for the Common Good

Leonard Joy
October 2011

—Quaker Institute for the Future Pamphlet 4—

Published for Quaker Institute for the Future by *Producciones de la Hamaca*, Caye Caulker, Belize <producciones-hamaca.com>

ISBN: 978-976-8142-32-0

How Does Societal Transformation Happen? Values Development, Collective Wisdom, and Decision Making for the Common Good is the fourth in a series of Quaker Institute for the Future Pamphlets: Series ISBN: 978-976-8142-21-4

Producciones de la Hamaca is dedicated to:

—Celebration and documentation of Earth
    and all her inhabitants,
—Restoration and conservation of Earth's
    natural resources,
—Creative expression of the sacredness of
    Earth and Spirit.

Contents

Foreword

There is a pervasive sense in our society that we are in a bad place and things are getting worse. The economy is failing to provide adequate support for a large and increasing number of people. The financial system is not working for the common good and is in danger of repeated collapse. The legislative part of the U.S. government is unable to function effectively. State and municipal governments are retrenching and cutting important services. Biodiversity loss is accelerating under the corporate mandate of economic growth, and the resilience of planetary ecosystems is shrinking. More and more there seems to be a system failure in both economy and governance that is radiating into almost every aspect of societal and environmental functioning.

This study by Leonard Joy, a veteran of international economic and social development work, is aimed directly at the kind of societal transformation required to stop this slide into catastrophe and begin to advance the growth of security and well-being for human communities and the whole commonwealth of life. More than half a century of experience on the frontlines of development research and fieldwork, plus long involvement with collaborate decision-making processes, has given Leonard Joy a particularly keen insight into the dynamics of how societal change happens. His insights are both necessary and timely. With our help, and with increasing recognition and implementation, they might also be sufficient.

Disruption and dysfunction are pervasive elements of contemporary economic and political life. With increasing economic turbulence, environmental degradation and social inequities, it is now ever so much more important to speak of societal transformation. We need to ask what conditions and processes could help build economic and social life into resilient, equitable, and ecologically sustainable communities, regions, and nations. We are better equipped than ever to envision the path forward.

A dysfunctional and failing financial system lies like a blowdown of smashed and tangled trees over the pathway to societal betterment. In addition, the pathway itself is washing out in the continued downpour of environmental destruction. Further to all this, the ecological and financial deficits are now joined by a democracy

7

deficit. Many governance systems seem unable to respond with moral insight and the collective wisdom of the common good. The question of societal transformation has now become much larger, encompassing the governance system as well. This goes to the root of public life. Whatever the particular focus of our human and environmental betterment work, the logic of our situation must now include a concern for the way the governance system functions and fails to function.

According to Leonard Joy's well seasoned vision, this integrated task requires moving into the next phase of human values development where the world is seen not as "a problem with which I must cope" but as a "creative project in which I want to participate." It is a phase of development where managers give way to mediators, captains of industry become facilitators of developmental design, competitors become collaborators and lobbyists speak up for unquantifiable values. Movement in this direction constitutes a transformation in both the kind of person a society promotes and the kind of society individuals promote. Emerging out of this reciprocation would be a transformed set of values embracing equity, integration, actualization and service; communication would take on an ethic of honesty, sincerity, comprehensibility and truthfulness; and, congruent with a keener sense of complexity, there would arise an appreciation of interdependency, an impulse toward generosity, and a respect for thresholds, limits and boundaries.

Not everyone concerned can pick up the whole package of this integrative task, but rapidly increasing alliances of support from every sector of human and environmental betterment have already begun to do so. Here is where Leonard Joy's concise and well focused study performs a valuable service. He sees individual values development as a prototype for societal transformation. He helps us understand the progression of human values development and the associated dynamics of societal transformation. He helps us to see both as a progression through which we are but half way and to appreciate that the next step is both hard and beautiful. He challenges precepts of international economic development advancing instead a practice of societal development implemented with attention to opportunities for human values development that serve as underpinnings for societal change. And he coaches those who are willing to embody transformative values in their skills, actions and practice.

He advances a deeper understanding of sustainability by recognizing moral imperatives–higher-order values–evident in the astute observation of social and environmental relations and thus inherent in the trajectory of human values development.

But his thesis is also a warning. By clinging too long, too obstinately, to the power and privileges of an outmoded phase of societal development, we play the caterpillar that refuses to become a butterfly. The caterpillar will die if it does not transform. Leonard Joy's message is that regression to authoritarianism is the alternative to advancement, certainly as the prelude to death. To help us understand and advance the metamorphosis of societal transformation, we now have this important study and its manual for the practice of collaborative discernment and effective decision making for the common good.

Phil Emmi
Professor, City and Metropolitan Planning
University of Utah

Keith Helmuth,
Secretary of the Board, Quaker Institute for the Future

October 10, 2011

Preface

There is a legitimate concern for transformative change in the way we live. Some see it as essential if we are to prevent an irreversible degradation of the environment and increasing social strife. Indeed, there are those who see even our species' survival at risk. We might hope that such fears are exaggerated. It is clear that we are caught up in powerful currents that will require a capacity for rapid and wise responses to avoid environmental and societal breakdown.

This pamphlet proposes a way to understand how societal transformation might come about. It does so by showing how individuals become transformed, how societal transformation follows this same process, and the action required to promote it. It looks at the process of personal transformation arising from an epiphany that produces a developmental leap and sees it as a special case of personal development. Even for an individual, the demands it makes on the reconformation of personal identity and behavior are seldom, if ever, met in an instant, and such sudden reconformations are hardly to be expected of society. Thus, in this pamphlet I focus not on sudden transformation as a goal, but on accelerating and guiding transformation as a process that includes inquiring into the role of the individual and what our understanding of personal development says about societal development.

I start from the proposition that we need to accept responsibility for the future of the planet and our specie's role in it. I seek a society that values human dignity and acknowledges humans as co-evolving and interdependent with the whole of nature. This pamphlet does not attempt to describe what such a society would look like. Indeed, I believe that design is a process of choice and elimination according to value-driven principles in light of an evolving context, rather than a plan to which conformity is required. This pamphlet emphasizes the importance of being sensitive to discrepancies between societal norms and processes, and those necessary for sustainable human and overall development.

In advocating for sustainability and the transformation to higher values that it demands, I do not discount the need to pursue minimum standards of material development—for secure livelihood, healthcare, and education for all. Active attention to these concerns is both an expression of core values needed for sustainability and the necessary basis from which higher values can build. But the values expressed in the way that these concerns are addressed is critical to their values development impact.

If, with me, you wish to accept responsibility for our species' future and that of the planet, we shall need a shared concept of human development that will guide our behavior in response to where we are and the possibilities confronting us. Above all, we shall need to be clear about the values that should guide us on our collective path. I invite you, the reader, to reflect on the inquiry described here and to examine how this reflection affects you. Does it bring a change in, or clarification of, your worldview? Does this in any way shift your attitudes or behavior?

The thrust of this essay is that there are moral imperatives, values, that are beyond culture, that can successfully challenge cultural mores and institutions, and that human progress is in fact marked by challenges to culture and institutions through identifying, asserting, and acting upon these values. Further, it is the possibility of our failure to identify, assert, and act upon these values that threatens our social and environmental sustainability.

This essay was first written with the support and encouragement of Tom Callanan of the Fetzer Foundation to whom I express my grateful thanks. Others to whom I wish to offer my thanks are Keith Helmuth, Phil Emmi, Charlie Blanchard and Shelley Tannenbaum who have contributed with insight and support. My special thanks and appreciation goes to Judy Lumb and her urge to perfectibility.

Leonard Joy
October 10, 2011

CHAPTER I
Development of Individual Values
A living systems perspective

When a living system fails to interact adaptively to its environment, it dies. Living implies a process of continuous structural accommodation in response to interaction with context. This response to interaction triggers learning, development and co-evolution. Adaptation to changes in context needs to be significantly rapid to ensure survival. Turnbull's account of the Ik (a tribal people suddenly displaced from the environment where they had learned to live) graphically exemplifies a society's failure to adapt to a sudden change in context.[1] Comparable examples of individuals who were, and who were not, successful at surviving such a challenge can readily be found. Individual and context co-adapt to one other—individual to society, society to changing individuals.

We in the West are sometimes challenged—collectively as well as individually—by sudden changes of context. These may indeed be formative. Consider the impact of the two world wars. But even without such traumatic events, the daily challenge to our worldview and its implications for the moral choices we make defines who we are. In either case, it is the responses we make, what happens when we reflect on these responses, that is formative—developmental. As we develop in this way, our values system changes.

This pamphlet is premised on the view that:

- Values are expressed as priorities reflected in our choices and behaviors.

- Values develop; they develop as higher values build upon lower values.

13

- Societal transformation involves a progressive shift in lived values along this developmental spectrum.
- We mature as individuals as our values develop.
- A broad path of values development is a potential common to us all as humans.
- Individuals, societies and the human species develop in a process of co-evolution.
- A minimum level of values development is needed to characterize individual, organizational, and institutional behavior for us to sustain the environment, human society, and progress on the developmental path of the human species.
- Shifts in the values supported by current human organizations and institutions depend upon individual values shifts.
- An understanding of how values shift occurs in individuals and societies is helpful in understanding how societal transformation, development, may be promoted.

The concept of transformation

The individual and societal transformations that concern us need to be understood as behavioral changes reflecting shifts in the lived values of individuals organizations and institutions.[2] These need to be shifts to higher—more developed—values. For individuals, such shifts can be gradual or, exceptionally, sudden. It is an inherent property of self-organizing living systems that change is continuous. So our concern is not how to promote change but how to promote transformational change in the directions that we desire.

How are we to understand transformation as applied to individuals and society? On the stage, a transformation scene is one in which everything is suddenly different: the pumpkin becomes a coach, the mice become horses majestically drawing the coach, and Cinderella becomes a princess dressed not in rags but in shimmering elegance. We do not expect this sort of transformation from society.[3] Individuals, however, have experienced life-changing transformations that may have relevance for societal change. We start by briefly considering such sudden individual transformations.

Miller and de Baca[4] have explored the impact the experience that transformative events or epiphanies has on individuals. These events are characterized by profound insights that trigger sustained changes in awareness of the self in relation to the world, a shift in personal values, and, consequently, of behavior.[5] They find such epiphanies, and subsequent sustained behavioral change, to be relatively rare. Most significantly, they suggest that epiphanies presuppose a readiness for their insights to be received and that the consolidation of transformation following an epiphany may occur only gradually. An epiphany is therefore a sudden step in a transformational—developmental—process. Given that the speed of progress in the developmental process is a continuous range, they decide against differentiating epiphanic transformative experience as a distinctively different developmental process. What is different is the complexity and extent of the constellation of perceptions that changes at once.

Supported by these findings, this pamphlet will treat transformation as a step in a larger developmental process regardless of how speedily it occurs. Rather than seeking the means to effect complex ramifications of instant change, we shall assume that it is not necessary for many things to fall into place all at once. But it will be sufficient if we can address lynchpins that can free the system and catalyze successive ripples of change.

For our concerns change must be developmental. It must result in new behaviors accompanied by a new higher level of values that support sustainability; and changes in the individual's relationship to oneself and to others must be observable. This implies constellations of perceptual shifts, such as changes in the self-identity of the person, not simply isolated changes in specific perceptions or behaviors. There are two milestones on the values development path that mark critical transitions, and which may be seen as especially transformational. In the first, personal transformations shift the norms of relationship of the individual to the other. The second, societal transformation, shifts the norms of relationships between people, and between individuals and society, as these relationships are mediated by institutions—especially government and the economy.

Human development as values shift

How do individuals and society interact to attain a level of values-behavioral development necessary for the collective purposeful pursuit of desired global futures? For individuals, organizations, and society as a whole, we are as we relate, both in the moment of relating and as a pattern over time. Our relationships to ourselves, to others, and to the cosmos define our state of development.

Our development is not measured by:
- how much we know,
- or how much we produce,
- or how much we have,
- or by how much we consume from the world;
- but by what we value as expressed in what we do—how we relate.

Living systems co-evolve. The history or developmental path of an individual—ontogeny—is a history of the individual's interaction and co-adaptation with its context. The history of a species—phylogeny—is a history of the species' interaction and co-adaptation with its context, manifested as evolution. As human society evolves, its developmental process can be traced, described, and assessed by reference to behavioral norms. Humans progress (or fail to progress) along a dimension of relational values. But there are many human societies and sub-cultures, and the history of their complex differentiation and integration is a key aspect of human phylogeny.

The path of individual transformation—development[6]

The following are propositions about personal development:

- Individuals change through their life span as they interact with their context, influenced and constrained by their personal genetic inheritance.[7]

- An individual's values evolve through two stimuli: (1) desirable or undesirable experiences; (2) conscious reflection that becomes significant only after a degree of development.

- An innate desire to belong initially encourages us to conform. Thus, our values are also "programmed" by our social experience and the norms that it offers us.

- All individuals proceed through similar developmental patterns, characterized by a succession of achievements in several interdependent areas of competence. Individuals vary in

16

the balance of their achievement in these several dimensions so that individual development paths are unique.[8]

- One dimension of development involves the psyche on a path of transformation through definable stages of self-awareness and self-perception.[9]

- This path of values development proceeds as a dynamic of integration and supercession rather than a continuous linear path. Clusters of key values mark milestones along the path.

- One stage builds on another. Attainment of each stage requires a re-conformation of self and a reordering of values. Even an epiphany, in which worldview and values can leap stages, requires time for consolidation into new personhood.

- A critical step in development comes at the beginning of reflective self-awareness and internal self-directedness.

- The progressive, or relatively sudden, achievement of lived higher values is the mark of development of the individual. Either way, it is transformation—the focus of our current interest.

Values development is the indicator of both psychic and overall personal development. It has the highest value as a primary dimension of the personal development path to which other dimensions of development contribute. It is more significant to our concern for societal transformation than any of the other dimensions of human development. However, the achievement of other competencies— instrumental, empathic, social, imaginative, and systems skills—is necessary to and supportive of values development.

Values development reflects a change in the nature of the relationship that a person has with self and with an increasingly larger sense of other.[10] When this comes from reflective self-awareness, it indicates an individual on a spiritual path with attainment of spiritual development.

We are primarily concerned with values as a dimension of development. There is great consistency in the findings of researchers regarding the nature of the development path and the stages through which it progresses.[11] It makes sense to speak of a person as being more or less developed as observed by his/her attainment on that sequence.

Hall and Tonna have identified an inventory of 125 specific values arrayed from lower to higher and valid across cultures (*pp. 20-21*). Hall followed up by describing the process by which we move through these and mature as individuals. He also inquired into the dynamics of values shift in groups, and applied this understanding to the practical task of shifting the values of organizations.[12]

The transformation that we need is one of human maturation through a process of reflection and internalization, a process of development that results in a significant progressive shift in lived values essential to support the sustainable development of humanity on Earth. Values shift in individuals (at least one person and then many) is a prerequisite to the institutional changes in governance and business that are fundamental to the societal transformation that we seek. The chief burden of this inquiry is to explain how the shift in individual values changes societal values.

Our biological nature

Before further considering the path of personal development, a few words on our biological nature are in order. Our development from embryo to fully mature is not simply a process of growth. We acquire cognitive, physical, and other skills that allow us to respond and adapt to our context.[13] These processes are driven by our emotional and feeling experience. Our survival depends on our ability to discern and discriminate between what nurtures us and what threatens us. We are programmed for self-preservation, to be discerning in a complex, today often unnatural, world.

We are also programmed to be sociable creatures, as seen especially in our capacity for love and shame, both of which have a role in sustaining us. The capacity for shame, however, is a double-edged sword since, while it motivates conformity, it may also cause separation, and separation is the root of conflict.[14]

In society, we learn, or fail to learn, how to manage our emotions. Being tired, stressed, under threat, drink, or drugs, we may regress to aggressive or other primitive behaviors. When such behaviors become learned as part of our characteristic behavior, we consider them delinquent, immature or even pathological. Greenspan[15] examines the consequences of failed emotional upbringing and its consequences for delinquency. The eneagram explains personality development as a consequence of early learned responses to fears and pleasures. All these observations have a bearing on the understanding of personal behavior and social phenomena, especially on the understanding of pathology—individual and societal.

The process by which we mature from pre-consciousness to autobiographical self and beyond is partly determined by emotions.[16] We attach life experiences, and the emotions to which they are coupled, to metaphoric representations that we use to categorize situations to which we need to respond.[17] These govern our worldviews, and thus our values[18] until they are confronted by inescapable challenges and/or by deliberate self-reflection. Thus are formed our attitudes to capital punishment, abortion, the free market, and on and on.[19]

Our values development is governed by our evolving worldview, which proceeds in a series of cycles that successively incorporate and advance from the values of the previous cycle (*pp. 20-21*). Each cyclical advance begins with an internal shift in our perception of who runs and directs our lives. In the first three cycles of our lives we are largely outer-directed by authority, whether it be that of parents, church, rules, or laws. Beginning in fourth cycle, we become increasingly inner-directed in all aspects of our lives. The transition to the fourth cycle marks a critical shift in our relational behavior, one that is seen here as transformational and vital to planetary survival.[20]

The core values sets[21] that characterize the major developmental phases are self-preservation, self-worth, self-actualization, truth/wisdom, and ecology/global.[22] The different individual worldviews of each of these phases may be encapsulated successively as:

1) The world is an unknown over which I have no control.

2) The world is a problem with which I must cope.

3) The world is a project in which I must participate.

4) The world is a mystery for which we must care on a global scale.

	"The world is a mystery over which I have no control"		"The world is a problem with which I must cope."	
Phases	Phase I **SURVIVING** Pre-conventional	T1	Phase II **BELONGING** Conventional	T2
Stages	**1** Safety	**2** Security	**3** Family	**4** Institution
	GOALS			
Values	Self Interest/Control* Self Preservation Wonder/Awe/Fate *See Appendix	Physical Delight Security	Family/Belonging Fantasy/Play Self Worth	Belief/Philosophy Competence/ Confidence Play/Recreation Work/Wealth/Value
	MEANS OF ATTAINING GOALS			
Values	Food/Warmth/Shelter Function/Physical Safety/Survival	Affection/Physical Economics/Profit Property/Control Sensory Pleasure/ Sexuality Territory/Security Wonder/Curiosity	Being Liked Care/Nurture Control/Order/ Discipline Courtesy/Hospitality Endurance/Patience Friendship/ Belonging Obedience/Duty Prestige/Image Rights/Respect Social Affirmation Support/Peer Tradition	Achievement/ Success Administration/ Control Communication/ Information Competition Design/Pattern/ Order Duty/Obligation Economics/Success Education/ Certification Efficiency/Planning Hierarchy/Order Honor Law/Rule Loyalty/Fidelity Management Membership/ Institution Ownership Patriotism/Esteem Productivity Reason Responsibility Rule/Accountability Technology/Science Unity/Uniformity Workmanship/Art/ Craft
Steps	**FOUNDATION**			**FOCUS**
	0 1 2	3 4 5	6 7 8	9 10
Cycle	**1** Authoritarian	**2** Paternalist	**3** Manager	**4** Facilitator

"The world is a creative project in which I want to participate"	"The world is a mystery for which we care on a global scale"

	Phase III		Phase IV	
T2	**SELF-INITIATING** Post-conventional	T3	**INTER-DEPENDENT** Global Ethics & Morality	Phases

5 Vocation	6 New Order	7 Wisdom	8 World Order	Stages

GOALS

Vocation	New Order	Wisdom	World Order	
Equality/Liberation Integration/ Wholeness Self Actualization **Service/Vocation**	Art/Beauty Being Self Construction/New Order Contemplation Faith/Risk/Vision Human Dignity Knowledge/Insight Presence	Intimacy/Solitude Truth/Wisdom	Ecology/Global Global Harmony Word	Values

MEANS OF ATTAINING GOALS

Adaptability/Flexibility Authority/Honesty Congruence Decision/Initiation Empathy Equity/Rights Expressiveness/Joy Generosity/ Compassion Health/Healing Independence Law/Rule Limitation/ Acceptance Mutual Obedience Quality/Evaluation Relaxation Search/Meaning/ Hope Self Assertion Sharing/Listening/ Trust	Accountability/Ethics Collaboration Community/ Supportive Complementarity Corporation/New Order Creativity Detachment/Solitude Discernment Education/ Knowledge Growth/Expansion Intimacy Justice/Social Order Leisure Limitation/ Celebration Mission/Objectives Mutual Accountability Pioneerism/ Innovation Research Ritual Communication Simplicity/Play Unity/Uniformity	Community/ Personalist Interdependence Minessence Prophet/Vision Synergy Transcendence/ Solitude	Convivial Technology Global Justice Human Rights Macroeconomics	Values

FOCUS				VISION						Steps
10	11	12	13	14	15	16	17	18	19	20/21	

4 Facilitator	5 Collaborator	6 Servant	7 Visionary	Cycle

21

The values shift that we need if we are to give purposive direction to our future must take our society into the third phase of this progression and beyond.

Values development reflects a change in the nature of the relationship that a person has with self and other. Values development is accompanied by the individual self identifying with successively larger wholes: from family and affines, to clan, tribe, nation, humanity; or, perhaps from family to ethnicity, school, nation, humanity. Such entities define for the individual the meaning of "common good." People tend to adopt the values of the communities, organizations, and societies to which they belong.[23] Somewhere in that progression there might also be place, nature (local to global), Earth and cosmos. As shown in the table, goals-values (e.g. self-realization) are distinguished from means-values (education) and 21 steps in their development are identified.

Lakoff has much to say about worldviews. It seems that we live by metaphors! A new picture is emerging of how we come to understand the world and how we behave as humans—especially how we derive the moral basis for our judgments and actions. We interpret the world in terms of our bodily, emotional, and relational experience and our moral sense—our sense of what is good—derives especially from our beliefs about what constitutes an ideal family. Two core ideotypes, with many possible variations, the "strict father" and the "nurturing parent" influence our sense of self worth. Along with other key metaphors, they provide the basis for our worldview and our responses to a very wide range of issues and situations.[25]

What we learn from epiphanies

Miller and de Baca contribute valuable insights into the nature and process of values shifts through the study of epiphanies. The quantum change that results in a positive transformative values shift can be characterized by "decentering from self, an abrupt move away from an 'I-me-my-mine' self-centered view of the world." Becoming inner-directed, not relying on what one has been taught to believe, but on one's own direct experience results in "a new, dramatically reorganized identity." In exploring the nature of the subsequent values shift Miller and de Baca found that:

"A common thread running through the stories is that, after such an experience, people often view the material world as merely a small part of a much greater reality, and a relatively unimportant part at that. This insight does not send them into monastic withdrawal from society. To the contrary it often inspires their devotion of significant time to compassionate service for others. Nevertheless, to reject materialism (in the philosophic as well as hedonistic sense) is to challenge the very assumptions on which a consumer society is based. ...

"After quantum change, particularly of the mystical type, few values lagged so consistently and profoundly as that placed on material possessions. ... Among ranked values, the acquisition of wealth often fell from first place to last. ... It was just that they were no longer attached to them, possessed by them. Anxiousness or envy for what is not gave way to awareness and gratitude for what is."

The positive experience was accompanied by a deep sense of unity with humanity at large and with nature:

"...experiencing, in essence, that love is what we are and what we are meant to be. It is our nature. ... Finally, across quite diverse experiences, a common experience was that all people are somehow linked, intimately and profoundly. ... We are not alone, separate, isolated beings."

While this is the direction of values shift that we should promote, we do not need, nor can we expect, so complete and radical a shift for societal transformation. Nor does everybody need to experience even the minimal degree of shift necessary to move us collectively forward on the development path. But who and how many need to shift are important questions.

In addition to their analysis of the nature of quantum change Miller and de Baca explore how and why change occurs and ways in which positive change might be supported. Their findings are important when we come to consider societal transformation. They discover that in individual transformational experience:

"Strained and separate aspects of identity are reordered in one brilliant moment. The deck is reshuffled. Pieces are moved around, and at some level the person suddenly sees how they can be rearranged into a new picture of self. Crisis is resolved by that person becoming someone new."

Miller and de Baca identify the following preconditions for individual transformational experience:

- *Breaking point*: ("the most common antecedent") a state of intense pain or emotional distress, a point of desperation or hitting bottom, life-threatening depression, disabling fear.

- *Deep discrepancy* between the actual self (who I am) and the ideal self (who I ought to or would like to be).

- *Personal maturation*: whether consciously or subconsciously, a constellation of contradictions is resolved. "a maturational phenomenon ... consolidation of wholeness and identity ... a reorganization of reality perception is then admitted to consciousness where it seems to come 'out of nowhere' but is understandably recognized as deeply right or true."

- *Sacred encounter*: The immediate experience of the divine and "[the] sense that the divine is always present, always seeking us and desiring relationship. ... One need not, however, believe in a personal, anthropomorphic God to postulate an encounter with the divine. Within various spiritual traditions, people are believed to have access to a great pool of collective, ancestral wisdom, akin to what Jung called the collective unconscious."[26]

Is the transformational experience unique to extraordinarily intuitive or self-actualized individuals? No, transformational experience "does not seem to be at all restricted to extraordinary, fully developed human beings. ... [Q]uantum change is not a phenomenon that happens only to intuitive people."

How can quantum change—transformation, development—be supported? Miller and de Baca suggest the following:

- *Supporting reflection*: "[R]eflective listening (accurate empathy, active listening) in particular helps the person to explore his or her own experience and to progress further along in the journey. The helping process is not one of instilling wisdom but evoking it. ... The helping task, then, is to facilitate the discovery process, the experiencing of discrepancy *already present* in the person but somehow sealed off or dissociated in a way that inhibits them from triggering change."

- *Creating awareness*: "If salient awareness of this discrepancy (between 'how I am' and 'how I want to be or could be') is part of what triggers quantum change, then there may be ways of heightening or facilitating such awareness."

- *Providing reassurance*: Affirmation that it takes courage to strike out in a new direction, to become a different person.

- *Normalizing*: suggesting that the changes experienced are normal.

- *Fostering hope*: "to affirm the capacity of the human spirit to change, even and especially when things look darkest."

- *Providing positive models*: "To see the positive possibilities in each other is a remarkable gift. At life's turning points people need positive possible selves to whom they can turn. ... Parents, friends, teachers, healers, clergy, social groups—all may suggest images of how one can be, the possible selves from which one may choose when a *kairos* is reached."

These ideas are all very relevant to the promotion of societal transformation.

Summary

Personal maturation or development can be traced as a path of values shifts accompanied by behavioral changes that manifest changing values. These reflect changing ways of relating to self and to other individuals, groups, the state, the environment, and the cosmos. Values shifts are themselves a consequence of changes in the ways we see the world and our emotional attachments to these perceptions. A key stage in development is reached when self-reflective awareness emerges with a concern for integrity and personal identity formation. In this stage, especially, challenges to worldview and integrity can lead to transformational changes in individuals over varying periods of time. While transformational epiphanies are possible, they are not common and cannot be evoked reliably, and the shift from passive re-perception to active acting on its implications may take time.

Progress—incremental transformation—comes from awareness of dissonance that leads to reflection on values and thence to a reconstellation of values and to behavioral change. Asking why makes values conscious; values are a powerful constructive force; reflection is the key to change. While crisis is a common precipitating factor, an outer crisis is not required for values shift. But today we are all in crisis and we should use it well.

The same path of values shift that is open to an individual may be traced for society, and for the species as a whole.[27] Further, we can be effectively purposeful in promoting that shift, and our focus should be on promoting societal self-reflective awareness to have the greatest potential for catalyzing transformational change.

The map of values (*pp. 20-21*) would help to advance us were we to share it. It would help us to be conscious, aware, reflective. It would help us to ground our joint reflection. It would help us understand where we are and the way ahead. It would guide activism. We need to see this map and ponder it together.

CHAPTER II
Societal Development from a Values Perspective

If we accept that our individual development is determined by what we value as expressed in what we do and how we relate, how could we not conclude that the same must apply to society? Such a redefinition of societal development concludes that a good society is one inhabited by people who relate well (according to higher values), to themselves, to others and to the environment—one that supports such relating.

We want the behavior of individuals and of groups to bring about healthy societal development: a maturing transformation that increasingly supports personal development. If the healthy development path of the good society recapitulates that of the individual,[28] it is one that leads to an increasingly moral society that supports the individual's development towards the higher end of the values spectrum.[29] Living this path fundamentally defines what it means to be human.

Reliable interdependence of the parts and the whole, and the absence of exploitative dominance by any part, is a necessary characteristic of healthy living systems. Mutual accommodation is needed not only between peoples but also between humans and the rest of the natural order. The morality that we seek is one that nourishes life and, specifically, our evolving humanity.

We can assess a society's development by the quality of relationships that it supports, by observing the stage of values development it has attained. As with individuals, we would observe differences between ideal, expected, and actual behavior. We would see individuals, organizations, and other social, political and economic subsystems in society, manifesting different norms and values that reflect their different stages of development. For each of these sub-systems, and the individuals comprising them, we could make valid statements of values maturation. Hall has developed methods for the analysis of business, religious, and not-for-profit organizations and a practice for supporting their values development. This analysis and practice may be generalized in principle to all levels of human collectivity.

Individual and societal transformation—the values connection

There is interdependence between the values of a society and the personal values of its individuals—individuals are formed in society but some, conforming less than others, aspire to higher values than those of the norms observed by society.

Living systems co-evolve and the history of an individual is a record of interaction and adaptation to its context. History is the record of the development path, both of individuals and of society, through their interaction and co-adaptation. Both individuals and societies develop (or fail to develop) from their responses to challenges and failures.

Change in individuals is induced by the need to respond to a changing context, which in turn, is under pressure from changes in individuals' actual behaviors and aspirations. Changes in individual behaviors affect society. Changes in society affect individuals. Society is a complex, adaptive, living system.

Since individual development and societal development are interdependent, societal development implies, and is dependent on, individual development. Individual development is in a degree molded and constrained by societal development, but only to a degree. Once an individual becomes reflective, the response to soci-ety's challenges is a matter of choice and an individual can choose to adopt and advocate norms that are higher than society's.

A major driving force in individual development is both con-scious and subconscious comparison of how we are with how we want to be. This engages our awareness of the world and when our perception of the world is challenged, our perception of who we want to be in relation to it is also challenged. "The usual route of change is that people operate on automatic pilot until they run into signals that something is wrong."[30] Changes may be limited and incremental; or they may be fundamental, transformative, and involve a major reconstellation of values that carries us to a new developmental phase.

One's awareness of incongruity between actual and aspired-to self—a lack of integrity—can be uncomfortable, even intolerable. Loss, pain, desperation or other emotional trauma can thrust such inescapable awareness upon us.

What is true for the individual is true also for society. A shared sense of crisis—precipitated by loss or by awareness of a new reality—can evoke a shared call to change. Crisis or not, many people may sense that something is wrong at the same time, leading to public questioning about what is wrong and what needs to change. Leaders may arise and articulate, or help others articulate, what is wrong and the called-for response. The pressure of public concern, of the perceived consequences of failing to respond to the new reality—or new perception of it—may grow. An acknowledged rightness and moral force of a call for change can lead to advocacy for new norms and actions, accompanied, perhaps, by accountability measures to strengthen their observance. This may involve the delegitimization of some behaviors and/or agreement about needed positive behaviors. Striking examples of de-legitimization can be seen in the abolition of slavery and the leadership roles of Wesley and Woolman, or the role of Gandhi in the abolition of the salt tax and the end of an empire. These are examples of response to reflection rather than to crisis.

The response to challenges will not always be positive. Some may resist, and cling to accepted familiar attitudes.[31] Rather than responding to challenge by maturing and adopting higher values, fear or material self-interest can lead to resistance, regression, even pathology. The alternative to responding to a challenge of awareness of interdependence with a larger whole, may be regression into xenophobia, paranoia, isolationism, and controlling/aggressive behavior. One individual might reconform into a higher self who becomes empathic and compassionate, discerning differently with whom and how to relate. Another might revert to a lower self with entirely different consequences. As it is within the individual where there is a tension between fear and love, between the limbic system and the frontal lobes, so it is in society with some holding predominantly one disposition and others holding the other. History is replete with societal examples of such regression.[32] But while our nature may dispose us to regress under pressure at early stages of maturity, we are not doomed if only we can advance to reflective levels of development.

Where there is a shift in reality or the perception of it, individuals may simply share their realizations with others who may in turn embrace them. They might join together to advance a shared concern and form a constituency around it. Until they do, their individual concerns may have little significance for societal change. History may be interpreted as the moral development of society through the working out of this process—the growth and impact of constituencies of moral suasion—over time.

A concept of human progress

There are significant implications of these understandings:

- The goal of societal development needs to be redefined.

- Material growth and technical advance should be seen as potential means to human development rather than measures of it. GDP does not measure human development.[33]

- Comparable criteria should be used for assessing societal and individual progress and pathology.[34]

- Stages on the path of individual and societal development are observable for analysis.[35]

- Continued progress—transformation—is a meaningful possibility, although there is the real possibility of stagnation, regression, and pathology.[36]

- Insecurity—especially the insecurity of poverty, as well as social exclusion, can inhibit values development and can prompt regression.

- Understanding what promotes values development in individuals allows projections of how values development might be promoted in society.

30

Currently there is resistance to these ideas rooted in the assumption that there cannot, and should not, be agreement about values—about what is right relating. This is rooted in the prevailing philosophy of freedom as the ultimate value and its presumed corollary: that we each are responsible for working out and living by what we each understand to be good; that it is not for anyone, certainly not the state, to impose values upon us.

Once we accept that there is indeed a universal, biologically based, human values development path, this philosophy is questioned. Indeed, we see the prevailing philosophy itself as reflecting a stage in our moral development, one that we might aspire to transcend. This reframing leads us to challenge our understanding of moral relativism. But it does not suggest that values can or should be imposed. On the contrary, it suggests that values need to be found by experience and reflection.

Society has developed

By this view of human development, there has been progress. Familiar examples include:

- the abolition of slavery, and of the salt tax in India
- abolishing segregation, capital punishment
- universal suffrage
- the increase of environmentally sensitive behavior

The past fifty years have marked significant advances in relational norms. Among recent significant advances, the abolition of apartheid and the creation of a Truth and Reconciliation Commission—linking individual and societal change through conversation—are especially notable.

Much contemporary progress can be linked to the existence of a Universal Declaration of Human Rights, which emerged from a crisis of conscience following World War II. Some one hundred and forty countries have ratified the Declaration. In countries where its conventions have been endorsed, there has been pressure to bring laws and constitutions in line. National Commissions for Human Rights and Ombudsmans' Offices have been created, as well as international accountability structures. To a greater or lesser degree, sensitivity to human rights violations, and accountability for

31

violations, have been enhanced. The overall effect on societal norms within countries and internationally has been positive and significant. The Universal Declaration, and the human rights education movement that it has spawned, has led to a growing social awareness of universal values. It has supported the growth and legitimacy of civil society organizations and constituencies, and provided an agenda of issues to be addressed.

Even where values shifts have begun, individual and societal internalization and change is not complete in any of the areas cited. Even in those places where the norms have been explicitly adopted and embodied in the law, norms are not reliably observed. Nor are people routinely held accountable for violations. But when accountability is expected, a norm signifies a level of values development. In this light, and with reference to the values development profile, there is evidence of progress that can be validated in many countries and internationally throughout history.

Examination of such examples as those cited reveals much that needs to be learned about the possibilities and preconditions of societal development and how it might be promoted.[37] Constituencies of moral suasion have been key to shifting societal values to progress, development, and transformation. They have appealed to individuals and revealed discrepancies between institutional or societal norms and what people knew to be good and right.[38] The developmental influence exerted by individuals and groups has de-legitimized personal and institutional behaviors and raised the standards of behavioral norms and ideals. However, in some cases, a similar dynamic has resulted in resistance to change, a regressive lowering of norms, and emergence of pathology.

Developmental arrest, regression and pathology

There are many features of our society that inhibit values development. The impersonality of so many of our transactions is but one. We are encouraged to believe that by pursuing a narrowly defined material self-interest, we will best serve the common good. We accept that it is appropriate for companies to induce us to go into debt that we cannot afford, or to buy things that do little to enrich our lives, or whose production or consumption may have harmful effects in one way or another. We submit ourselves and our children to acculturation to relational norms, which many of us would reject if we were aware of them.

Even in America, seen as the epitome of democracy, we are content to be governed by a system where decision-making processes are not conducive to the expression of collective wisdom, a system that offers little scope for effective participation, and where decisions are patently not "of the people, by the people, and for the people." Such systemic features are to be found inhibiting development all over the world. A living system in which the parts are not mutually supportive, in which some parts dominate and parasitize others is sick. In society, excessive power and its use for benefit at others' expense is a pathology to be addressed.

Summary

Societal progress is a valid concept. It is observed as advances in societal norms defined in terms of a universal values development dimension. It has resulted from people in sufficient numbers, depending on their ability to influence collective action, acting effectively to de-legitimize behaviors found unacceptable, or to promote new norms reflecting higher relational values in ways that succeed practically. Societal progress depends on self-reflecting individuals aspiring to higher values, finding resonance with others in this aspiration, and who, together, become an effective force for change. But progress may depend on first addressing pathology—the systemic reasons for our stuckness.

Societal transformation is inconceivable without the personal transformation of some people to inner-directedness, self-reflection, and concern for integrity—personal and societal. This step of personal transformation is the essential first step in societal transformation. But changes in individual behaviors will meet severe constraints to societal progress unless there are sufficient numbers unwilling to behave, or to have their governments or other agencies behave, as society now allows and expects. Institutional behaviors and mores will generally need to be questioned directly.

There is no doubt, for instance, that if it pays them, producers will respond to sufficient numbers of consumers who go organic, humane, and green. Changes in individual behaviors—boycotts, tax refusal, recycling, non-violent witness—in massive numbers could change some societal norms and behaviors. But transformation is impeded by our institutions. The economy, especially, constrains how we relate to one another and all our institutions contribute their formative influence on the mores to which we conform. Collective pressures will be necessary if we are to change our institutions and remove the constraints to continuing personal transformation.

To date, personal transformation has produced societal transformation when it has inspired collective witness for systemic progress. Absent steps to inspire, inform, and articulate collective witness, the simple promotion of personal transformation is an inadequate strategy for securing the changes we now need. Personal work on ourselves will indeed lead us to reach out to others and to volunteer in places like soup kitchens. Personal inner work will not, however, necessarily inspire in us the inclination to search deeper to address the underlying causes of the emergence of poverty. In order for this to happen, the individual needs to be part of a constituency with a worldview and practice for effecting both inner and outer change.

While personal transformation is essential to societal transformation, it needs to occur in community and to be sensitive to the way we live collectively, not just individually. It needs expression in witness, both individual and collective, for higher values and against violation of these values. Moreover, it needs to be guided by a view of the world that understands interdependence and society as a living system. It needs to understand what holds people in their present values—the unconscious metaphors they live by, the fear that the thought of change evokes, the mores that they are exposed to and expect to observe—and how to address these to support reflection and change. The drive for transformation needs to know which behaviors need to change.

CHAPTER III
Promoting Societal Transformation

A ddressing pathology requires making explicit the grounds for identifying and objecting to pathological features of our social institutions, articulating what should be, and how it could be realized practically. Pathology is to be found with imbalance of power and a failure of feedback and responsiveness to the deprivation of parts of society or the environment. In its crude manifestations we see it as tyranny, oppression, exploitation, coercion and arbitrariness. But it has subtler forms that are still pathological in spite of their being less obvious. Public dialogue is necessary to identify and press for needed change.

Success of moral activism depends on the readiness of a system for its perturbation by trigger events. There are circumstances in which moral activism will not take root. Sometimes the changes required are beyond the incremental and are truly fundamental, requiring widespread shifts in the architecture of societal relationships. Again, there may be agreement on values, but even the first steps to the change path may not be perceived. The cry may be for a shift far beyond a society's immediate ability to envision, or willingness to risk, or individuals' capacities for behavioral change. While crises (for example, loss of identity, and the need to redefine it) and a growing sense that things cannot or should not go on as they are, will contribute to a potential openness to change, other things are needed to precipitate change or lead to progressive values shift.

In order for their moral activism to become coherent and strategic, and thus perturb a delicate equilibrium to trigger change, people who seek change need to be able to conceptualize the socio-economic-political system, along with its flux and breaking points. They need to be intellectually and practically credible. They need to address the fears and attachments of those who are implicated in change. A vocal and credible constituency must call for others to join it rather than creating adversaries through confrontation and thus forcing separation. The constituency must live by the values that it is asking others to live by.

Development may be promoted by acculturation in healthy relational norms. Especially, too, the habits of self-awareness, reflection, internal direction and owned self-responsibility need to be inculcated. This requires that these norms and habits be lived by mentors in families, schools, clubs, churches, and supported by the media.

Creating the space for conversation and promoting a culture of dialogue is high on the list of strategic action for values development. Increasing the awareness of values and the role they play in all spheres of life will do much to support reflection, the awareness of dissonance, and the desire for change. The development and application of techniques for analyzing value structures and dissonances, especially to situations demanding organizational complexification and the integration of different cultures, increase awareness and give practical means for advancing values shift.

Both for individuals and society, values development is promoted by creating space for conversation and reflection about values and their implications for the way we live. These need to be supported by provision for monitoring the condition of individuals and communities, and feedback and response. There needs to be sensitivity to the human condition—personal or societal—and provision for responding to what becomes known.

Many people are engaged as change agents in organizational, governance, and societal change. Almost none of them have practices that are informed by an understanding of values shift and its significance for complex systems change. Few practice from an explicit basis of right relating in support of self-organization. Societal transformation calls for a community of practicing consultants and leaders informed by such understandings.

A level of values development is a prerequisite for reflective concern and examination of worldviews. Therein lies the rub. How many, in what roles, have attained to this level? Without reflective concern, the stimulus and challenge to values shift comes from unavoidable awareness of threat or from loss. How much loss, or unavoidable threats, must there be to catalyze the shift in worldview and values needed to carry us forward? And how can we overcome the fear of loss that would result in regress rather than progress? The challenge for moral activists is to build constituencies of moral suasion and to focus attention on creating readiness for cumulative significant change. Purposeful, moral activism creates this readiness and triggers perturbation. What it means to be effectively purposive is discussed below.

We can choose to be purposive

As we can individually create our own lives by the choices we make, so we can collectively create the history of the species. Indeed, we cannot avoid so doing. The only question is whether we wish to do this reflectively, deliberately, and together. It requires that we develop values-sensitive public reflectiveness to guide choices for public action. We need to form strategic constituencies of moral suasion and address those with power in society who continue to make choices based on narrow perceptions of national or corporate interest.

Our goal should be to promote a society where human rights values, and the responsibilities they imply, are reflected in relationships and institutions that express these values.[39]

We need a deliberate, collective, purposeful intent to frame a vision of the way ahead with values development as our goal. That intent needs to be developed and shared in a global conversation about who we humans are, where we are going, and who and where we want to be. Such a conversation is entirely possible if we engage in it while respecting both our cultural differences and our common humanity. We can start by exploring shared values and becoming sensitive to behaviors that offend these values. A shared concern for human dignity will carry us far in agreeing on what needs to change and how change needs to be promoted.

The Universal Declaration of Human Rights provides a framework and checklist of ways in which human dignity may be enhanced or violated. While there is room for interpretation, and while it is far from comprehensive in its values, the Universal Declaration of Human Rights points to that to which we need to be sensitive. It offers criteria for behavioral change and new relational norms. Perhaps even more importantly, it provides a basis for a growing global conversation.

Being effectively purposive

Our individual maturation—values development—may be promoted by a desire for integrity, by reflecting on how we perceive the world, how we are living in it, and our aspiration for the future. Similarly, societal development can be promoted by a desire for collective integrity, which includes collective sensitivity to, and collective reflection on, what is happening in the world; our individual and collective responsibility for it; and our aspiration for the health and development of the species and the planet. We must examine how we wish to be and become committed to observing the norms that this requires.[40] Individual maturation requires that the personal ego find its place in service to the common good, and societal maturation makes the same demand of collective ego.

Progress may start with one who articulates the way ahead. It may come from dialogue that engages different perspectives until a shared perspective emerges. But unless the vision spreads, it lies dormant and unproductive. Conversation is essential for creating and internalizing shared vision, for discovering what we have in common, what we share and our aspirations. Apart from, and in resistance to, coercion, it is the primary mechanism for the collective internalization of change.

From time to time conversations help some of us to discover ourselves individually and collectively, but such conversations are not woven into the fabric of modern culture. Indeed, pubs and churches no longer serve, as once they did, to sustain community of place, and television has largely replaced the hearth and usurped mealtime conversation.

Nor is there any clear vision of our aspired-to future, or even much concern to find one. Several commentators have remarked on a contemporary crisis of identity.[41] How often are deep conversations stirred and widely heard in public? Certainly, there seems not to be a deeply reflected sense of the direction we want to take. We lack effective processes for collective reflection on where we are going as a species, on what we want for our global future.

Indeed, there are issues-oriented policy review mechanisms. Professional bodies, churches and other groups meet to consider aspects of the human condition, but they seldom examine the economic, political, social-cultural dimensions of the global system as a whole in any depth. They rarely take values aspirations as their point of departure. Nor do they hold inclusive, public or face-to-face conversations in the spirit and culture of dialogue that educes collective wisdom. If we care for our future as a species, if we care for the future of Earth, we need a global weaving of conversations about these very things. If we are to be purposive together, we must create spaces where we have conversations about what it means to be human on our planet. This is critical to providing a basis for being collectively purposive.

As we become sensitized to and reflective of our values we will discover what it means to preserve our humanity. We shall discover, too, how deeply this is connected to our relationship to nature and to our physical environment. We shall become sensitive to the way our man-made environment affects the way we relate to one another.

Discovering our humanity in connecting with one another

The decisions that take us along the path of our historical destiny as a species, and along the path to environmental disequilibrium, are generally made from a dissociated rationality, from pragmatism, expediency, a misguided sense of self-interest, and compromise rather than from a sense of what we deeply know, value, and aspire to. There is a knowing that depends neither on evidence and measurement, nor the strictures of culture and the promptings of unconscious metaphor.

Some would say that what we need to be grounded in is the Spirit, "that of God within," or some other expression of the Divine. However it is experienced and metaphorized, what is asserted here is that there is a ground of being that we share as humans that we can all tap in to, and that we need to learn to tap into, individually and together. We will not agree on matters of taste or cultural expression, but when we are grounded in our humanity with our ego in its place, we will find resonance in our sense of the common good.

39

We may more easily agree on what violates our humanity than on what we need to do to nurture it. But ceasing to violate our humanity is much of what we need to do to nurture it. So the challenge is to ground ourselves, individually and collectively, in our shared humanity, to become sensitive to behaviors that violate our humanity, and to work to de-legitimize them.

We must start by bringing people together, creating the space where they may "know one another in that which is eternal."[42] This requires that we be willing to interact in ways that support such knowing. What might such ways be and what individual and collective skills do we need to develop for this to happen? We need to learn—and to use what we already know—about how to evoke collective intelligence and apply it to understanding and responding to reality.

We need to foster leadership skills for modeling grounded (Spirit-led), open systems understanding. We need to discover and practice finding unity through diversity. Cross-disciplinary dialogue and the inclusion of feminine perspectives are important elements of this. We need to develop ways in which the unity that is found in small groups becomes a unity of groups of groups, and groups of groups of groups. We need to discover and learn from examples of where this has been done.[43]

We need to reinvent democracy and learn how to use such democratic institutions as we now have in order to do so. We must work to change political and economic institutions so that they support democratic values. We need to be assertive in identifying and protesting violations of human dignity without ourselves becoming violators. This means that we must learn how to make our concerns heard in ways that express the values we aspire to, ways that invite others to listen with a willingness to change.

While change may be led from below, change generally requires that identified leaders' values become the shared reality of management groups and finally those of followers. Thus, whether it comes from above or below, leadership must be, in Hall's terms, one cycle ahead of the values expressed in the norms of an institution or society. Leadership provides space for reflection around values. It asks and seeks answers to the question: "Why?" The power of leadership to define our conversation may be observed in the way that current leadership has changed public conversation. Think tanks play a leadership role with ability to dominate worldviews and define the conversations. Think tanks are needed to support inquiry into societal transformation.

For our organizational capacities to advance, leadership needs to become a collective process, rather than a function of one person. As positive values shift occurs in an organization, the leader is an enabler, allowing others to function cooperatively.[44] Later, the leader becomes one among a group of equals with a common task. The mindshift in values, skills, and worldview—in behavior—occurs with the recognition that development, especially in the area of leadership, can occur only when there is a concomitant shift in processes and organizational structures that support them. We need to develop a community of support for such changes.

If the understanding of values development (and its metaphorical basis) on which this essay is premised is valid, it follows that there will be those who will not agree with our assertions of moral imperatives. Apartheid, universal suffrage, slavery, and civil rights are only a few of the issues that evoked widely divergent views. But they also exemplify moral challenges that were ultimately irresistible, even though not everyone initially agreed to the need for, or desirability of, change. The thesis of this essay is that there are moral imperatives that stem from our common humanity, that are beyond culture, and that can successfully challenge current norms and institutions. Identifying and acting upon these is the mark of human progress. Social and environmental sustainability is threatened by our failure to identify and act upon these moral imperatives, a concern that adds particular significance and urgency to the consideration of this thesis.

Changing the way we make collective decisions

The Quaker mode of decision making is but one example that demonstrates the possibilities of reaching decisions that tap into the collective wisdom. Quakers say that this happens when people are Spirit-led. But much may be achieved in secular situations if the following key conditions are met:[45]

- stated commitment to the common good,

- explicit willingness of all parties to acknowledge and support the agreed-upon legitimate interests of all parties,

- grounding all participants in the experience of their humanity, and

- ability to support open systems thinking.[46]

This includes, but goes beyond, the practice of dialogue. Particular skills are demanded of those who would lead such a practice of group discernment, including, for example, the skills demanded of a Quaker clerk. Special skills are necessary when not all participants have the same grounded sense of shared humanity, the capacity to put ego in its place (a practical substitute for wishing to be Spirit-led), and the capacity for guiding systems thinking. The development of such leadership skills and the development of a culture of dialogue must be priorities, if we are to deal effectively with the emerging global situation.

We need to meet the challenge of integrating cultures with different levels of development and cultural expression. When we look at the spectrum of values attainment of different societies and cultures, we find that none is reliably able to manifest the values necessary for our survival. Indeed, many are several developmental stages below the attainment of those values. We shall need to address the reality that behavioral norms are not at the level needed for our survival; that there are major differences not simply in cultural mores but also in the values that they reflect. We shall need to address these differences if we are to find social cohesion.[47] It will call for a deep engagement, wrestling with differences and diversity.

All societies comprise individuals at different levels of values development, and almost all countries are characterized by increasingly diverse ethnic cultures and subcultures, each exhibiting a range of individual values development. Integrating people of diverse ethnic identities and values development into a single governance system is a challenge in itself. As we seek to respect and observe human rights standards of treatment in relating to immigrants and minorities, we are faced with the demanding tasks of changing attitudes and norms, promoting inclusion, and finding unity through

42

diversity. These tasks are especially challenging in the face of religious fundamentalism that does not support listening with a willingness to change. In general, two–way communication between parties at significantly different levels of values attainment may be infeasible in some areas of discourse. But knowing one another as human beings may—given trust—reveal underlying values known and aspired to by all.

We each need to be aware of where our culture is on its historical path and what is an appropriate aspiration for incremental progress. We need to identify and respond to current societal behaviors that need to shift if we are to progress.

Changes in worldview

Our values are directly related to our worldviews. The publication of the King James' Bible, and the perceptions that Galileo, Newton, Darwin, Marx, and Freud brought to the world, significantly affected how people saw themselves relating to one another and to the cosmos. The worldviews of Ayn Rand or the Chicago school of economics have been hardly less significant in our day. Our biblical and latter-day prophets also challenge us to reflect on how the world works and who we are in relation to it. We sorely need this reflection and reframing of our role in this complex adaptive system of humanity on Earth. Society will surely change without it, but if change is to be purposeful, healthy and transformative, such reflection and reframing is a prerequisite. A values development perspective would significantly illumine such reframing.

Changes in skills

Values shift requires the development of new skills if we are to practice higher values both individually and collectively. Empathy, as a lived value,[48] requires a level of interpersonal functioning that generates imaginal skills needed for the systems awareness and systems skills necessary for lived means-values[49] such as "Mission/Objectives"[50] and "Corporation/New Order."[51] A whole range of instrumental, interpersonal, leadership, and systems skills needs to be acquired, while negative skills that involve "conscious and unconscious techniques that delay or impede a person's ability to take responsibility for his or her life" need to be avoided or abandoned.[52]

Summary

A key element of a strategy to promote transformation is the creation of constituencies of moral suasion. Such constituencies will arise from the experience of shared humanity and the identification and agreement on moral imperatives as the basis for unity with diversity. This calls for inclusive conversations reflecting on what is and what should be—how we want to be and relate—and on what it takes to promote shifts in societal norms and the processes and institutions that express them.

Specific changes in behaviors and decision-making processes will be identified and pressed for with emphasis on the need for ourselves as individuals to live the values we seek and the need for our actions to be congruent with these. This will mean seeking to recruit the support of those whose change is sought, rather than treating them as adversaries.

There will be times of flux that provide special opportunities for change. It is essential to be prepared for these with developed skills, capacities for non-violent action, and well-articulated objectives. Among the skills needed will be that of leading conversations to discern and find unity on the common good with understanding of the systemic implications of contemplated actions. Powerful support is needed from think tanks. They would provide factual and analytic monitoring of events, spread awareness, articulate concerns, objectives and goals, and offer coaching of individuals and groups. Not least, they could provide sensitivity to the metaphors underlying worldviews that need examination. The following chapter explores these points further asking "How can we act?

Chapter IV
How Can We Act?

We must build "constituencies of moral suasion," that respect human dignity and make demands for change so compelling that they cannot be morally or pragmatically challenged.[53] We need to consider how this might be done. We need to learn from history to become strategic in supporting societal transformation by pressing for the de-legitimization of practices and institutional behaviors that are unacceptable.[54] We can model new behaviors and organizational forms, envision futures, offer alternative worldviews, philosophies, and metaphors, make explicit and challenge those unconscious metaphors that are not supported by our best understanding.

We have noted how embodied metaphors strongly influence our behavior and our level of values development. When combined with Hall's understanding of the problems of bridging values gaps, we can see that dialogue among people who hold different underlying (generally unconscious and unexamined) metaphors may be fruitless.[55] We need to examine the validity of these metaphors if we are to behave with responsible awareness. The "strict father" and "survival of the fittest" metaphors that are so crucial to current worldviews and policy directions need to be made explicit. We must challenge their validity where they are instrumental to impeding societal advance.

In the past 250 years, a key challenge to society and the environment has been the spread of the market economy. Karl Polanyi is one especially articulate critic disturbed by the usurpation of society by the spread of the market economy and the effect that this has had on human relations.[56] Many see that today's global economy violates human rights, endangers the environment, and holds the prospect for increasing violation and degradation, as well eroding the role of government. The tension between Keynesian perspectives on the roles of government and the market and the, now dominant, worldview of von Mises, von Hayek, Milton Friedman and the Chicago school of economics is unresolved. Nor has it given rise to a new systems view that responds to the realities of the changing world economy. But the need for this becomes clearer every day.[57]

One challenging aspect of this reality is the increasingly disproportionate voice of those with economic power. They use that power not only to pursue self-interest regardless of the common good—albeit often in its professed pursuit—but also to influence significantly the worldview and values of the mass population in America and throughout the world. Our governance systems only weakly reflect values that support equity, inclusiveness, participation, subsidiarity[58], transparency, and accountability.

The sustainability of our economies is premised on continuing growth, boosting the consumption of the already affluent to sustain the demand for investment and innovation. But there is a limit to the burden that can be absorbed by the environment from indefinite growth.

Changing technology is also changing the demand for labor. Keynes' caution about the potential for "underemployment equilibrium" is becoming an ever more serious consideration in the economy of the future. Clearly, the nature of work is due for a fundamental change. We must explore ways that businesses might be motivated and organized to become more fully human and to become responsible for their citizenship roles in relating to society and the environment.

The economy we seek will support progress on the path of individual and societal human maturation. Our concern now is that in many ways the economy inhibits this development, disrespects humanity, and fosters pathology. The task is to examine where and how this is so, to identify the behaviors that are unacceptable and to indicate how they might be changed. What would a "values-respecting" economy look like? What would businesses look like if they behaved as corporate citizens, if they observed mature values in the way they expressed relationships within the business and to the world? What would the role of government be in relation to the market? How would an environmentally sustainable economy be itself sustained? How would the world look if the right to livelihood (for rewarding, meaningful, non-exploitative, work) were secured? What would be the motivations for work and enterprise? How would power in society relate to power in the economy, and how would we ensure that society was not dominated by undue concentration of power? We need to respond to these and other related questions with an unprecedented level of intellectual investment even beyond the present investment in articulating and justifying current dysfunctional political and economic philosophies.

Much of the world is influenced by the political philosophy now dominant in America. Sandel argues persuasively that this is a regression from that held by the founding fathers,[59] and Lakoff demonstrates that it is falsely justified by invalid metaphors of the strict parent family and misunderstood Darwinism.[60] We need explicit reflective public dialogue on our economic and political philosophies and their underlying perceptions and worldviews to assess how well they serve us and how they need to evolve. Values, worldviews, and operative metaphors are tightly interconnected. Values shift—societal maturation, development—will require them all to change.

Churches also need to mature. Religions that fail to admit of continuing revelation, the reinterpretation of worldview and values appropriate to the evolving context, will die or be transformed. Christianity, Islam, and Judaism are all under pressure in this respect.

Progress involves the incorporation and supercession of past values and their integration into a new whole. New worldviews, new values, and whole new ways of organizing thought, identities, and loyalties are coming into focus. But they have yet to be fully articulated and integrated. Systems analysis, especially living systems analysis, has done much to catalyze this revolution,[61] giving us a deeper appreciation of interdependence, co-evolution, societal health, and development that has begun to shift our values, our view of the role of humans, and to affect our ideas of how we need to relate.

Our understanding of biological systems and of who contemporary humans are, and where they came from, has been hugely extended by biological science during the past 50 years. The human species has, or is about to acquire, the technology to intervene in its future course if it so chooses. This technology brings a demand for heightened responsibility, for it comes also with the potential loss of social and environmental sustainability. We urgently need corrective measures if this is not to be our fate.[62] Never was there a greater Biblical "loss of innocence" or a greater need for those with this awareness to confront it.

Technological, social, political, and economic change present challenges in the way we relate to one another and the environment. Authors Jared Diamond and James Burke[63] are among those who have traced the impact of ecology and technology on the way society evolves interactively with the eco-technological context.

We are warned of the possibility of societal and environmental collapse.[64] Even should we be able to avoid this, we shall still be challenged to determine who we shall be as humans. Not the least of these challenges is the prospect of cyborgs—humans with artificially augmented or extended human characteristics and capabilities—blurring the definition of what it is to be human, even though they will have evolved from an unbroken autopoietic history.[65] Developments in genetics and biotechnology will be especially challenging, but they will not be the only technologies that will change who we are and how we relate.

The Universal Declaration of Human Rights has the potential to create an awareness of dissonance that has already proven to be catalytic of change. While it is not yet accorded the same status, the Earth Charter has similar potential. In endorsing these documents, in whatever degree, we accept that we all have political, economic, social, and cultural rights—and that these imply responsibilities to one another. It requires us to examine the various ways in which we collectively and individually hold these responsibilities. Acceptance of these responsibilities with an active concern for meeting them marks a level of values development that is not yet attained.

But accepting these responsibilities in principle is one thing; finding ways in which they may actually be met is another.[66] The first step is to become sensitive to, and acknowledge, situations where they are not met. We then need to determine and take responsibility for remedying the situation. In this way we give substance to our values and translate them into institutional norms that define our citizenship responsibilities, and provide for mutual accountability. In this way, we become our lived values.

Taken together, these considerations call for changes in our economic, governance, and justice systems that, however incrementally pursued, will cumulate in fundamental societal transformation that will be reflected in our education and health systems and in our family and community lives. The efforts of NGOs and international agencies to improve access to food, medical care, and education are significant for providing the necessary means to values development. How these means are promoted—the processes for programme identification, design, implementation, and accountability, the institutional structures and accountability criteria embodied—can, however, add or detract from their developmental impact. We need to be conscious not only of what we are doing but especially of how we are doing it.

Where change efforts might be most significant
We need to see where our energies are best focused if they are to be effective for change. Which issues have the potential to command the power of moral suasion to bring about change? Which are powerful examples of principles that have wide application and, once admitted, may bring widespread, systemic change?

A survey of present activist concerns would reveal just how much ferment there is.[67] It would also reveal how fragmented, issue-oriented, inarticulate, and lacking in overall vision or strategic sense much of it is. There are good reasons why it is out of fashion to draft utopian visions, but in the mind of a good deal of the public, the way ahead appears to be increased material growth, recycling, and community self-sufficiency. Yet it is clear that growth is not sustainable.

"Globalization" has become a particularly hot issue. Demonstrations in Seattle and Genoa that brought together activists with a range of environmental and human rights concerns may mark the beginning recognition of how much these different concerns have in common in terms of values, a common voice, and a strategic energy focus. However, the various protagonists' differing worldviews and metaphors need to become explicit subjects of reflection and dialogue. Moreover, while concern about the impact of globalization might well be a strategic and unifying focus, there is little evident analysis of where the various elements of concern fit within an overall strategy for change.

The strategies pursued by the major religions of transforming society by transforming individuals, by prescribing right-relating, has had limitations. Such strategies can get only so far with those who are outer-directed. When they lack a systems view, focusing solely on the individual rather than the context in which the individual is formed and constrained, they are themselves a barrier to change precisely because they do not support the inner authority of the reflective individual tempered in community. What is needed now is support for reflective integrity through conversations exploring dissonance informed by a systems view of our changing world. These conversations need to evoke all four of Wilber's quadrants— the personal and collective conscious and unconscious, and the individual and societal systems.[68]

If our central concerns are human dignity and maturation, our attitudes and activities, the means by which we pursue our values-directed goals, must be consonant with the values that we espouse. There is much to be learned from the history of non-violent protest.[69] The issue is one of effectiveness, as well as integrity. A strategy for transformation must include building capacity for effective non-violent witness.

So, while prioritizing of issues for public attention is vital, securing public attention and focused awareness on these is the objective. This takes us to the issue of how to engage the public in informed conversation about societal development. Given the power of the media and the concentration of its control, we must strategize to engage the media and the public. Today, the internet is our prime resource.

Model what is possible and broadcast it
We seek changes in the way we live: new styles of business, new monetary systems, new "green" technologies, new ways of promoting public dialogue, new practices of collective intelligence, new forms of participatory governance. We need experiments with each of these and those that are functional and enduring must be

spread. We already have models to develop and apply,[70] but these need to be made accessible and broadcast.

We need to invest in think tanks—to publish, initiate and contribute to vital conversations and people's attention[71] to the separate strands of concern and activism[72] that need to be woven together. What we aspire to be draws us forward to higher lived values. We need a vision that not only rejects what we know to be unacceptable, but also generates models of how things need to be if they are to nourish life.

What this might mean in practice

Much of what is needed is already going on. Institutions and groups are wrestling with these concerns and trying to bring them together to explore where each fits in the larger picture. The World Wide Web supports our connecting and drawing upon one another. But the weaving function that finds and expresses the collective voice, that plays the role of the Quaker clerk to express the collective sense, to discover those things around which there is unity, is not well established. We lack a process for exploring vision and strategies for moving ahead. Similarly, while there is ferment in the exploration of group process and collective intelligence, it needs to become more coherent and more collectively discerning as a process of conscious societal learning.

The United Nations, especially the United Nations Development Programme (UNDP), has a potentially significant role in modeling how to bring a human-rights-values lens to bear on economic, social, cultural and political concerns and in designing public and private action to address them. While charged with this responsibility by the UN Secretary General, the UNDP is only slowly coming to grips with it. It needs support and encouragement. This capacity is particularly needed if we are to reverse the approaches based on the prevailing philosophy of economic development and management-by-results efficiency.[73] If both multilateral and bilateral international agencies are to engage as partners in developing capacities for values-directed self-governance with all that means for relinquishing control and conditionality, a new mindset, new skills, and new management philosophies will be needed.

The institutions that powerfully influence our worldviews and norms—schools, churches, the media—need to be challenged. We need institutions committed to building an aware global citizenry. This implies openness to learning—to reflecting on worldviews and values. This means that they must walk their talk, being prepared to change in the process. Key churches and religions, especially, will not find this easy, but they will not be able to support personal transformation unless they themselves are willing to be transformed.

We need public conversations that are informed dialogues rather than adversarial confrontations, engaging all who are willing to observe a culture of dialogue, all who are ready to listen with a willingness to change. They need to bring into dialogue the many different perspectives of the business sector, government, and civil society.[74] The experiences of many small groups—local to global— need to be brought to synthesis to reveal where there is agreement and where there are issues that need further resolution. Above all, the impact of such conversations needs to be heard and felt in governance decision-making processes in all sectors.

History shows us that in setting out to influence the path of values shift to promote sustainable human development, we need to practice what we aspire to, especially inclusion, the essence of human rights.[75] We need to understand that, while higher values can be promoted and nurtured, legislation will not of itself change values, as the experience of prohibition amply demonstrates. We need to build from history with step-by-step development through the values spectrum and find ways to take account of differences in levels of culture, values, and world views.[76] Moreover, we need to promote healing to overcome the traumas of history and dissolve the barriers to love and common cause. We need to avoid fault-finding and address the system instead of attacking its actors. We need to promote shifts in ideal, expected, and actual behavior, working at all these levels to bring about behavioral change.

The role of philanthropy in recovering our humanity

A major challenge to foundations is to support "putting the pieces together." If there is value in the thesis of this pamphlet, it comes from the integration of the understandings of several disciplines and perspectives, thus creating a map by which we can conceptualize the nature of our development path, and what it means to become responsible for it. When these various understandings are brought together they create a new understanding that is needed to support societal purposefulness. The map they provide needs testing conceptually and in application. Its elaboration will give rise to many questions that will need to be addressed. The conclusions reached from this new worldview will themselves call for support for specific activities. Foundations are challenged to come together to find their strategic role in support of these developments.

"Putting the pieces together" is seen as essential in the sense that no one approach will have significant impact if carried out in isolation from the others. Worldviews, metaphors, skills, leadership and overall values awareness need to go together and be addressed at individual, collective, and institutional levels.

Investment is needed in big picture analysis. There are so many different points for intervention to support human progress. But some interventions and some constellations of interventions will be more significant than others. Supporting informed conversations, building networks of conversations, weaving syntheses of conversations, and supporting the development of a culture of dialogue and co-intelligence, seem basic.[77] Support is needed for the articulation and declaration of a non-party, non-partisan public voice on what needs to be and what needs not to be, along with modeling, testing, and broadcasting the learning from experience of new more life-giving ways of organizing. Support is especially needed for a global conversation among people bringing their humanity to the discourse. People need to engage this conversation, not as representatives or as advocates for anything, but simply as themselves. What is needed is not a summit but the convocation of groups, of groups of groups, and of groups of groups of groups.

Much is already happening.[78] But efforts are fragmented and not generally informed by the values development perspective offered in this pamphlet. This seems critical because the adoption of this perspective changes things. Especially, it offers criteria of progress and guidance for action. But it is the explicit awareness of, reflection on, and engagement with each other around what we believe and value that is the key to change. Strategic action will focus on social situations manifesting what Miller and de Baca describe as critical preconditions for transformation ("breaking point," and "deep discrepancy") as presenting both opportunity and special need. They will apply Miller and de Baca's suggestions for supporting transformation: supporting reflection, creating awareness, providing reassurance, normalizing, fostering hope, and providing positive models.

Foundations have exercised great influence in the dissemination of ideas. One example is the support given to Frederick von Hayek to bring together thirty-six disciples of von Mises; the impact of that meeting on the development of the Chicago school of economics, and the effect that this has had upon the history of the world. Today, foundation-supported think tanks are devoted to extolling the virtues of the unconstrained market, justifying the value of competitive natural selection, the strict parent family, and derived worldviews on foreign policy, capital punishment, gun control, welfare, health systems and the rest. They exert a powerful influence on the popular mindset. The point here is not the validity of these views, nor even of the need for bricks-and-mortar think tanks; but the significance of the role that foundations play in choosing to underwrite these or other perspectives, and the responsibility that they bear for human progress.

Challenging current development concepts

In contemporary mainstream approaches to promoting development, priority is accorded to economic development—growth—to increasing average per capita income, generally seen to derive from modernization. Stated goals generally qualify the growth/modernization objective in a variety of ways (e.g. "redistribution with growth, ... sustainable growth with equity,")[79] and the goals of elimination of poverty, sustainable livelihood, participatory democracy, environmental protection, freedom, and choice are commonly explicit. But there is a general presumption that economic growth is the overall goal and the means of achieving these subsidiary goals. Indeed, the presumption is that the objective of social policy must be to maximize society's total material wealth so that the choice of what to do with it is maximized. It presumes that our humanity can find greater expression the greater our material wealth.

But this is not informed by an understanding that the economy itself is a domain of relationships that does not now reflect or support

54

the relationship values necessary for societal development as understood in this pamphlet. Worse, inasmuch as relationship values are expressed in the concern for developing social capital, it is because social capital is seen as necessary for economic development. There is little or no consideration of the possibility that the market economy—as now experienced—erodes rather than supports society and social development, or that growth may not be sustainable.

The call by the UN Secretary General for all UN agency activities to be directed through a human rights lens, should, in principle, do much to move us toward a values reorientation. The Universal Declaration of Human Rights expresses a high level of relational values that, if it were truly to provide the driving values of the UN agencies and the countries they serve, it would indeed promote a values-developed society. However, the understanding of these values implications within technical assistance and aid agencies has not yet penetrated deeply into even the UN agencies' approach to development. This is true even of the United Nations Development Programme, which has as its goal "sustainable human development."[80] The full implications of "human rights mainstreaming" are still to be internalized and development is still seen as economic development.[81] Seeing it instead as values development would make a fundamental—transformative—difference to the way the UN agencies operate and assess their performance. Public prompting at all levels, local to global, is required to raise awareness and change what is being done.

So what's new?

None of the separate ideas offered here is new—though few of them are common currency—but together they offer a way of looking at the world that has the power to change how we live in it.

The idea that societal progress might reflect the development path of the maturing individual is hardly new. The idea that all humans share the potential for a development path of the maturing individual, and that it can be traced in a path of values development, has yet to be accepted either as a theory or as an observation of practical consequence. Assimilation of these basic ideas would fundamentally change how we address concerns for people today and for our future as a species. They would displace material growth as the development goal and instead offer values development as as framework for the design and appraisal of development efforts efforts in the context of concern for the environment. But widespread awareness of and sensitivity to values and their development would constitute a significant shift in worldview.

The idea that human progress can be traced as a history of change brought about by moral suasion in the context of changing technology and environmental pressures is not new, but it does not drive our collective conscious.

That our governance systems are defective, is widely understood, or at least suspected. The idea that they should be the targets of serious examination with intent and willingness to work for fundamental change has not penetrated public consciousness. Truly participatory governance is beyond elections. That Robert's Rules of Order are obsolete, obstruct the emergence of collective intelligence, and are incompatible with values that we shall need to adopt if we are to progress, is hardly a subject for discussion, let alone acceptance as a priority for activist attention. While there is reference to citizenship, the concept of citizenship and its applicability not simply to individuals but also to collective entities—to businesses, churches, universities, and the organs of public administration. This theme needs to be taken up more strongly.

The United States' political philosophy has gone off the course that the founding fathers set for it, and it is in urgent need of review, but this does not seem to be generally disturbing.[82] The free market has been reified, and how to use the market to support society, rather than displace it, is not a question under serious discussion.

Putting these questions on the forefront of the agenda for purposive change, and in the context of the propositions offered here, is new. Understanding the force of misguided metaphors that support our dysfunctional political philosophy, and the idea that we need deliberate strategies for public reflection on them, is not new, but it is hardly widespread. In the larger context of the constellation of ideas offered here, it takes on a new strategic significance.

These ideas are to be distinguished from a proposal for yet another religious revival. Yes, the major religions have promoted values for millennia. But they have not promoted maturation. With the qualified exception of Buddhism, they have promoted ortho-doxy and obedience to external authority, thus inhibiting develop-ment. Moreover, they have focused on the life and behavior of the individual without attention to the formative pressures of society—including its churches. They do not have a systems understanding of society. And, always granting exceptions, the lived values of their churches were survival oriented, authoritarian, and paternalistic—the lowest end of the values development scale. They have not per-formed well as learning communities. The approach offered here is one of self-discovery, in community, of mature human values inher-ent in us all.

It will be noted that the present pamphlet does not see societal transformation to depend on the attainment of higher levels of con-sciousness. We have much unused capacity within our current level of consciousness and an ability to know that we too seldom tap. Global transformation does not require us to do more than use the conscious states already available to us. Whether or not there are possible higher levels of consciousness is not the issue. They simply are not needed, nor is the drive for their attainment a plausible strat-egy for societal transformation.

Many ideas are in the air. They fall into place when we adopt a living systems view and a new focus linking ontogeny and phy-logeny, seeing the path of human development as a path of values development. It produces an epiphany that, widely shared, has the power to change who we are. The complex web of relationships that is who we are will not change instantly nor will it change speedily, but change will reverberate around our living system and the change will ultimately be transformational.

Epiphany has the power to change how we act. A living sys-tems understanding of how the parts relate to the whole in a process of healthy self-organization, co-adaptation, and development is an epiphany that would point us to how and where we need to act in order to regain health and set ourselves on a resilient and sustainable path of human development. It indicates the capacities that we need in order to express and integrate our diversity rather than generating resistance and conflict in the process of suppressing, compromising, and homogenizing our differences. By explicitly identifying and sharing the values that will take us forward, we will reveal what so many different concerned and activist groups have in common, so that together they will find an irresistible common voice.

While not, by far, the only response that will be called for, the power of moral suasion has been demonstrated through history. Without question, it has commonly been backed by other forms of protest and withdrawal of legitimacy and other measures will likely continue to be needed. But a moral sense of rightness is the necessary, and powerful, basis for protest. The next chapter sets out group skills for tapping into our collective intelligence—for creating a culture of dialogue. They are long-practiced, well-tested skills of Quaker discernment that have also been successfully applied in secular contexts. We need to practice these skills.[91]

CHAPTER V
Collective Intelligence

The previous chapters have noted that advancing our values demands the acquisition of skills. Critical among those skills now needed are skills that can draw upon our collective intelligence. Robert's Rules, so pervasively applied, are ill designed to tap our collective intelligence and do much to explain our collective inability to discern and pursue the common good. The fact that adversarial debate fails to respect all needs and legitimate interests—and, at best, provides for compromise—is fairly readily grasped. Where not all voices are equally heard, the neglect of some concerns may be acute. And where there is no mutual caring between parts and whole there is pathology, even death.

But even when it is understood that inclusion, equal voice, and non-adversarial discourse is desirable, this understanding proves inadequate to tapping the wisdom of the whole. Of recent years, there has been considerable attention to the management of meetings, and a number of different approaches to collective decision-making are now available. These variously emphasize fostering creativity (brainstorming), educing the full range of participants' stories and perspectives, facilitation that captures and builds upon the various contributions, nurturing a culture of respectful attentive listening, avoidance of negativity and fault finding, structuring a process from brainstorming to analysis and the elimination of less than effective responses. We have "open space," "world café," "appreciative inquiry," "integral public practice," "dialogue," "goldfish bowl," and a host of patented techniques and checklists for running effective meetings. Fetzer's report *Centered on the Edge,* which explores the essential conditions for tapping into collective wisdom, notably draws little on these. Neither does its conclusions suggest that any of them would be found to meet all necessary conditions in which collective wisdom is arrived at. Indeed, the report could be read to suggest that these conditions still elude us. Such a conclusion would be unduly pessimistic, because there are many examples of sustained decision making in which collective wisdom prevailed using the Quaker practice of decision making.[83]

The fact that this process is approached as "a meeting for worship for business," raises the question of its more general applicability but approached as a meeting for discerning the common good, the practice stands up well in secular contexts.[84] The spirit of what Quakers do, in discernment of the common good, is eminently accessible to all. The challenge lies in leading those whose daily habit of mind and state of values development is not of the Quaker disposition and their habitual meeting behaviors not those that they need to manifest if they are to participate in the discernment of collective wisdom. Here the connection between individual and collective transformation becomes apparent. The following sections are the essentials of Quaker practice, translated where necessary into secular terms.

Grounding of all participants

Quakers start their business process with a period of silent worship in which they aim to center[85] themselves in that of God within or, in the case of universalist Quakers, in the sense of loving kindness to—and identity with—all creation, or, in the case of Buddhist Quakers, in the compassionate, non-attached, no-self. In so doing, what they all have in common is that they are putting their egos aside to serve the task rather than using the task to serve their egos. They are also opening to the awareness of the larger whole, the greater good, and they are inwardly joining together in holding the meeting community in their care.

All this derives from a culture held and evolved over the past 350 years. This is not something that can be expected from those who are not party to this culture. In many cases, however, it is possible even in a secular context to hold a few moments of silent recollection of the gravity of the business in hand and centering in the spirit in which all are enjoined. Even where this seems difficult to invoke, it is possible for a tone to be set at the beginning of business and for agreement to be reached that the meeting is to discern and serve the common good. For those at early stages of values development, it may not be immediately possible to aspire to more than the search for "win-win" solutions to problems. But even this may be enough to start, to engage people ultimately in an appreciation of, and desire for, the common good and to lead them, beyond tolerance of those that they would not join, to a sense of mutual appreciation and concern. And it is possible to require that the ego should serve the task and not the other way round and expect people to be mutually accountable in this regard.

Ensuring that all voices are heard

It is the task of the clerk—or facilitator—to ensure that all voices are heard. In a Quaker meeting it is understood that all voices will be heard and that there need be no competition to be allowed to speak.

Respect for all persons

A tone may be set and held by the facilitator of respect for both the participants in the meeting and those outside who will be affected by the decision-making process. The facilitator must be given support from participants in holding one another accountable. It may be given to understand that participation is contingent upon maintaining a code of conduct with its principles made explicit.

In secular situations it is important to make the legitimate interests and concerns of all parties explicit, agreed, and subject to the explicit commitment of all to uphold. The goal is to move beyond this agreement to mutual caring, but simple acknowledgement and respect will go a long way to supporting the emergence of collective wisdom.

If legitimate interests and concerns are made explicit, hidden agendas become easy to name and to call into question. Should such a situation arise in a Quaker meeting, there would be a call for silence to search for a Spirit-led way ahead.

None of this should ignore or deny the necessity for trust. In situations of existing extreme distrust, the possibility of progress is likely to depend on providing for accountability. Our prime concern here is our inability to be wise together, even where there is no overt enmity and antagonism. Even in such situations, there may be an underlying fear of loss to be calmed. The ability of the clerk/ moderator/facilitator to earn everybody's trust is essential. All must feel that their publicly claimed legitimate interests will be heard, respected, and protected.

Maintaining community—loving relationship

In a Quaker meeting, a decision is never a victory for one view or another. A good—Spirit-led—decision is one that not only results in sound practical consequences, it is one that maintains the loving community. Even should there be those who cannot unite with the decision arrived at, they are nevertheless willing to stand aside trusting the wisdom of, and maintaining their love for, the meeting. The function of the clerk is critical in ensuring the articulation of dissent, of making sure that it is fully received, felt to be truly heard, and "labored" with. Then the readiness of the meeting and dissenters to move on to a minute of decision can be assessed.

Speaking out of the silence

Quakers use silence to punctuate a meeting to allow for such grounding. In secular contexts, it is likely to fall primarily to a facilitator to be sensitive to the need for grounding[86] and to help people to ground themselves in what they are feeling and the roots of their feeling. This reflects an underlying understanding that there are powerful and—when tested in community—reliable ways of knowing that do not depend on rationality. Helping people to tap into what they know makes particular demands on a facilitator's skill and training.

In a Quaker meeting, ideally at least, silence is allowed after each contribution to allow it to be fully absorbed and to allow subsequent contributions to flow from a grounded state. This is perhaps the greatest challenge in changing the habits of secular discourse because it requires a state of being personally grounded.

Sensitivity to interdependence—open systems thinking

A major task of a facilitator is to support open systems think-ing. This implies understanding the wider context in which a con-cern—and the sought for response to it—arises. It requires becom-ing clear about the system under concern and the implications of interdependence and feedback as it affects the good of the whole.

Addressing the clerk not one another

The effect of addressing the clerk is to reinforce the sense that each contribution adds a new piece or perspective to the total picture rather than canceling or trumping others' perspectives.

Speaking simply

This is about the avoidance of tricks of speech designed to bully or obfuscate with sophisticated rhetoric or to impress by weight of words. In secular situations, a facilitator may ask for brevity and avoidance of repetition and, as necessary, summarize the essence of an overblown presentation and check with its author that this was an accurate summary. While, in non-Quaker meetings, several people might feel the need to amplify and underline a contribution that they agree with, Quakers wishing so to do will respond with "This Friend speaks my mind," thus assisting the Clerk to gain the sense of the meeting.

Speaking one's own truth, without advocating that all should act on it, is about contributing to a greater understanding rather than attempting to confine the understanding to one perspective. Each is seen to hold, potentially, a piece of the truth and all contribu-tions have their place in the collective perception of the greater truth. Appreciative inquiry is a secular practice that emphasizes the need to focus on what should be, rather than on diagnosis of what is wrong.

Commitment to air dissent

Unity—the essential goal—is not possible if some withhold dissent, especially if there is intent to subvert or subsequently disown a decision. Openness is essential. Truth is seen to emerge from consideration of all perspectives. Establishing this as a shared understanding and commitment requires explicit discussion where it is not to be taken for granted. The norm that solidarity is expressed by withholding dissent is turned on its head. The task of the facilitator is to make it safe for people to express dissent.

Equality of voice

Encouraging equality of voice is a way of separating ideas from their authors and avoiding bias that might come from the influence of status.

Being authentic with the expression of feeling

Authenticity is key. Authentic, grounded expression comes with evidence of the emotion behind it. This is not simply appropriate and permissible; it is what has to be. But any simulation of emotion in order to affect others is entirely inadmissible and should be discouraged and discounted by the facilitator.

Threshing meetings

Not all meetings need be designed to arrive at decisions. Where decisions are complex or where they are likely to reveal major differences of feeling or understanding, preliminary meetings to air these differences and to hear from one another may be desirable and help the process of mutual understanding. Quakers designate such meetings as "threshing" meetings that serve to air feelings without the need to make any decisions.

Factual and analytical material

Decisions need to be informed by data and analysis and provision is needed to prepare this and for its critical review prior to embarking on decision making.

Role of the clerk

The Quaker Clerk attempts periodically to summarize the state of the collective perception as the decision-making process evolves. This is a way of testing the degree of convergence and divergence of perceptions and revealing where the picture is still less than clear. This is progressively modified until there is unity. While this should pose no difficulty in secular situations, it is not always an accepted role of secular meeting facilitators.

Among Quakers, there arise situations when, having labored with dissenting Friends, there seems no immediate hope of resolution of differences. Where immediate decision is avoidable, and generally where decisions are weighty even where there is no dissent or evident unease, Quakers allow time for "seasoning" a decision to allow for further reflection and for unease to surface. But there are times when decisions need to be made and action initiated. The role of the Clerk in sensing the willingness of the meeting to proceed is critical. The guidance offered to clerks in such situations might well be adopted in secular contexts also.

It is helpful, even essential at some point in the process, to structure a discussion in a sequence in which aspects of concern may be considered according to some necessary critical path while expecting nothing to be resolved until the picture is whole. Both clerks and facilitators have a key role in this and in making clear what constitutes relevance at any time.

Decisions made by unity

Friends do not vote or act on the will of the majority. In Quaker experience, it is possible for all to unite in a decision, even when some have reservations. A united meeting is not necessarily of one mind but it is all of one heart. This may be too high an expectation in secular contexts, but a willingness to settle for compromise can be antithetical to seeking wisdom. Moreover, in a secular context, it may not be easy even to secure the willingness of a minority to stand aside. While there are those whose concerns are not reflected in a proposed decision, the work of discerning wisdom needs to continue. This is likely to hinge on securing agreement about the legitimacy of concerns and on the consequences of alternative decisions for sustaining community. Compromise is only acceptable where legitimate concerns are otherwise irreconcilable.

Larger organizational structures

It is one thing to secure the wisdom of a gathered group of people, it is another to find the collective wisdom of hundreds, thousands or millions of people. The Quaker structure involves Monthly, Quarterly, Yearly meetings and General Conference. The process by which concerns may emerge at any level and evoke the response of the whole has proven effective in providing for inclusion and the manifestation of collective intelligence even where large numbers of people are involved. While it is true that the participants in Quaker process are self-selected for a willingness to observe the culture, effective leadership can do much to promote it and to call forth collective wisdom.

Connection between individual and societal transformation

The behavior expected of those participating in meetings for the discernment of collective wisdom is that reflective of a significantly high order of values development. The question arises: "How is the requirement of inclusiveness consistent with the requirement of such behavior when not everyone is living the values required?" It is possible for the leadership provided by a moderator/facilitator/ Clerk to secure observance of such behavior and appreciation of its value to all. But this presupposes not simply a high order of moderating skills but also a level of values development from such leadership. This highlights the importance of developing such leadership capabilities in individuals and of their taking up leadership roles. The effectiveness of collective decisions depends on the actors' ability and willingness to walk the talk and to be held accountable for this.

A culture of dialogue fundamental to collective wisdom—co-intelligence—and participation in such dialogue will have transformational impact on individuals as well as society. The values learned in dialogue will be expressed outside the public forums in which they take place. They will provoke reflection and reflection fuels the engine of transformation. Forum processes and moral constituencies will be mutually reinforcing. As they have impact on institutional values, constraints on individual development will be eased. Increasing numbers of individuals will advance into higher levels of lived values and propel society forward. The connection between individual and societal transformation is synergistic. Collective decision, and the values expressed in the process of its making, affect the individual. Individual and society both advance and constrain one another.

Endnotes

1 Turnbull (1972)

2 "Human values are the qualities that are evaluated high on the list of an individual's priorities." (Hall, 2006, p.25)

3 Turning points in society may be observed but they do not mark completed transformations and not all are developmental. Consider: the visits of the Pope and Margaret Thatcher to Poland and their impact on the rise of Solidarity; the fall of Marcos in the Philippines. In each case there was some degree of continuity and a subsequent, protracted, process of reconformation. With the collapse of the Soviet Union, there came a hiatus—a complete collapse of individual, organizational, and national identities. The "rules" by which people related to one another were no longer in effect. But they were not readily replaced by an alternative set of "rules," institutions or national identities. This was not an example of transformation. The old living system died, it did not metamorphose into a higher state; the structure of its complexity was destroyed and needed to be rebuilt not only in each of the new national entities, but even in the structure of interpersonal relationships. The same might reasonably be said about the earlier transition into the Soviet Union. Russia, at least, is still an authoritarian state.

4 Miller and de Baca (2001)

5 Scrooge is a classic example of an epiphanic transformation, as is Paul on the road to Damascus. Miller and de Baca (2001) examine documented individual cases.

6 In addition to the sources referred to in this essay, topics and author viewpoints that would be referenced in expanded writing would include: Armstrong (2006), Cox (2005), Csikszentmihaly (1993), Fowler (1981), Gellner (1992), Helmuth (2003), Korten (2005), Layard (2005), Potter, *et al.* (2001), Rand (1952), Sheeran (1983).

7 Individual development from infant to mature adult, is a process of transformation in which the transitions to successive stages of maturation are, generally, barely noticeable without close scrutiny.

8 Wilber (2000) summarizes the literature on psychological development. He shows how the various contributions together describe a broad framework of multidimensional psychological development in the individual. He notes dimensions of this development that are, in varying degrees, interdependent on one another.

9 Documented by Wilber (2000) and Hall (2006).

10 The highest level of reported values achievement is characterized as one in which "the world is a mystery for which we care on a global scale." (Hall, 2006)

11 Wilber (2006) offers a comprehensive tabulation of the development stages described by many researchers. It is significant that,

in studying individual transformation, Miller and de Baca (2001) analyzed the values shifts of the subjects studied and produced their own values array and developmental sequence that has high consistency with the findings of both Hall-Tonna and Graves.

12   Also in Hall (2006). Beck and Cowan (1996) also supports this thesis. Hall's significant achievements are in making values development observable and elucidating the dynamic of values shift. The Appendix gives definitions of these values relevant to values in the context of a business organization.

13   Maturana and Varela (1998)

14   Scheff (2000)

15   Greenspan (1997)

16   Damasio (2000)

17   Lakoff and Johnson (1999)

18   Hall (2006), Wilber (2000) and Graves (2004).

19   Lakoff (2002)

20   Table, pp.20-21

21   Twenty-nine of the 125 values are seen as core values with other goals-values and means-values are clustered under these.

22   Ecology/global: aspiration to take authority for the created order of the world and to enhance its beauty and balance through creative technology in ways that have worldwide influence.

23   Bellah et al. (1992) explore the tensions experienced by individuals whose workplace, church, and home make different expectations of their behavior. Gergen (1992) graphically depicts how different they can be.

24   Lakoff and Johnson (1999), Lakoff (2002)

25   Elaboration of these ideas would explore the implications of family and evolutionary metaphors together. I would illustrate with regard to such issues as: genocide, international HR courts, capital punishment, affirmative action, attitudes towards caring for the marginalized, health service provision, economic and political philosophy, governance, and environmental management.

26   Miller and de Baca (2001)

27   We accept Margaret Meade's premise that we are one human species with common potentialities.

28   This has been the argument of authors such as Elgin (1993) and Barbara Marx Hubbard (1993) who see us now as in a state of adolescence.

29   While the Hall-Tonna schema is only one version of the values development dimension, it exemplifies the body of literature on the

subject—a body of findings with remarkable consistency—and one that has been applied to achieve values shift. Wilber (2000) provides an overview of this literature.

30 Miller and de Baca (2001)

31 As we have seen with the events of 9/11, solidarity in the assertion of who we are and how we usually respond to crisis could be a response-inhibiting reflection and change.

32 It is not difficult to illustrate this from contemporary history but a prime example would be the regression of Germany after Versailles.

33 The "mainstreaming" of human rights called for by UN Secretary General, Kofi Annan, goes much of the way towards an implicit redefinition.

34 Note, too, that this measure is not of the advancement of science.

35 This concept, once forcefully rejected as fallacious historicism by such eminent and persuasive writers as Popper (1954), Berlin(1991)—even Aldous Huxley (1959)—is under review. Wright (2001) offers one interesting contemporary critique.

36 Note the parallels with the concepts of stasis, incremental evolution, and punctuated equilibrium in evolutionary theory.

37 History also shows us what does not work. To generalize briefly: means need to be congruent with ends. One needs to live democracy not simply legislate for it; violent revolutions are not effective in securing brotherhood, peace and justice.

38 This raises the subject of "ways of knowing." Knowing is not only a matter of data, fact, or reason. It is especially an appeal to something within, a gut understanding that appears to be part of our shared humanity.

39 I refer here to the values implicit in, underlying, the *Universal Declaration of Human Rights.* However, the Declaration does not cover all aspects of needed values development. In particular, with reference to the environment it needs to be supplemented by the *Earth Charter.*

40 This is not a universally shared view. Indeed, several commentators (Anderson, 1997) argue that integrity and consistent identity is unnecessary and ill-adapted to modern society, that we should learn to develop and live with the ability to conform to each of the various cultures that engage each of us, that societal development will be characterized by increasing breadth not simply of the permissible range of expression but also of the values that these differences reflect. This view, while clearly rejected by the present essay, needs examination, but this is left to a later expansion of this essay.

41 Charles Taylor (1989)

42 Old Quaker injunction.

43 The development and integration of levels is critical. Quaker processes and structures have much to offer here.

44 Heifetz (1998)—essential reading on leadership—clearly brings out the advanced values required for effective leadership.

45 See Chapter IV.

46 Open systems thinking: Awareness and understanding of the interdependencies within the larger context in which any concern is embedded. Here, the relevant systems are those that bear on aspired-to values.

47 Beck & Cowan (1996)

48 Empathy: Listening and responding to others so they see themselves with more clarity, seeing and feeling their concerns and issues as they do.

49 Means values are instrumental for the achievement of goal values. However, it is possible to have only means values.

50 Mission/Objective: The ability to establish organizational goals and execute long-term planning that considers the needs of society and how the organization contributes to those needs.

51 Corporation/New Order: The skills, capacity, and will to create new organizational styles or to improve present institutional forms in order to enhance society.

52 Hall (2006)

53 This is the conclusion arrived at also by Falk (2000). "Realist morality continues to underpin global security, providing widely acceptable moral rationalizations ... for recourse to force and for stretching the law opportunistically in the relations among states. Such behavior is characteristic for both hegemonic leading states and dissident states. These rationalizations for the use of force include opposing aggression, preventing nuclear proliferation, upholding a balance within a given region or protecting a particular state, containing or promoting the spread of Islam, ending Western domination and secularization, resolving ethnic and territorial grievances, and promoting independence and justice. Humanitarian morality, embodied in various ways in different ... constructions of a "human rights culture," exerts only a marginal influence, one that is uneven, media dependent, and generative of shallow commitments; in this regard global security structures and processes give only lip service to humanitarian morality.

"For humanitarian morality to underpin global security it would be necessary for drastic shifts in world order to occur, principal among them a reigning in of state/market forces and a rise of transnational social forces that embody a nonviolent ethos. Tendencies in this direction cannot be ruled out, although their present prospects appear to be in virtual eclipse. It is possible, however, that within the next decade or so, the economic, ecological, and cultural pressures of inadequately regulated globalization-from-above will generate acute alienation of sufficient magnitude as to create new revolutionary opportunities, including those that would mount a ... challenge to realist morality as the basis of global security. ... Whether such resistance will turn into a ... movement dedicated to the drastic reform of global security and an insistence on humanitarian morality will perhaps be the most profound question of the next hundred years."

54 There is much to learn from such sources as Ackerman and Duvall (2000) that exemplify and analyze experience with non-violent resistance and teach us that, as individuals, we must walk our talk.

55 Fruitless unless at a profoundly human level and even then without a shared view of the world.

56 Polanyi (2001), see also Baum (1996) for a brilliant synthesis of Polanyi's work.

57 The series on Daniel Yergen's book, *The Commanding Heights*, broadcast by public television, clearly reveals the challenge posed in this institutional domain.

58 Placing effective responsibility as close to the level of the individual as practicable.

59 Sandel (1998)

60 Lakoff (2002)

61 Capra (1954) and Harman and Sahtouris (1998)

62 McKibben (2006)

63 Diamond (2005) and Burke (2007)

64 McKibben (2006)

65 I am grateful to Philip Payne for this observation and our discussion of Maturana's ideas on this subject.

66 But the experience of the Netherlands in securing covenanting to explicit environmental responsibilities by both private and public actors gives hope of this possibility.

67 Ray and Anderson (2001), Ray (2002), and Hawken (2008)

68 Wilber (1995). It is worth noting here that Quakers are among those who maintain a conversation about values dissonance, personal and societal. They have indeed had significant impacts on our institutions through moral suasion. But they do not collectively engage in the deep understanding of societal change at the level to which I believe the conversations need to be elevated.

69 Ackerman and Duvall (2000) and the video series that accompanies it.

70 See, among others Hawken, *et al* (2008) for "green" technologies, Hock (2000) for forms of participatory governance, and Lietaer (2002) for a discussion of money. Tom Atlee's website <co-intelligence.org> and his *Tao of Democracy* have compendious references on the subject of collective intelligence, and the *Faith and Practice* of any Quaker Yearly Meeting encapsulates 350 years of experience in tapping collective wisdom (try e.g. Philadelphia, Pacific, or Britain Yearly Meetings' versions). The Netherlands' experience with environmental covenanting and Swedish experience of "The Natural Step" also point to effective models for change James and Lahti (2004).

71 See the Rockridge Foundation <metaphorproject.org> for changing metaphors. The Institute of Noetic Sciences <noetic.org> and the Kettering Foundation <kettering.org> both support local forums but neither operates to address these issues in a systematic and cumulative learning process.

72 Activism needs to be expressed as both personal and collective behavior that witnesses to what we know to be right-relating.

73 Amartya Sen has proposed freedom with choice maximization as the development objective (UNDP *Human Development Report* 2001 <hdr.undp.org/en/reports/global/hdr2001/>). But these are means and to what end? Neither these nor the also proposed 'well-being' or 'happiness' equate to—or ensure—the goal of sustainable human development.

74 Note that participants need to engage as human persons not as representatives of a point of view or particular interest.

75 It is important here to observe the distinction made by Hall between goals values and means values. Inclusion expresses: equality of regard, unity, participation, subsidiarity, community, transparency, and accountability (mutual responsibility).

76 The possibility of societal epiphany is surely worth exploring but the feasibility of such an epiphany being sustained and translated readily into the needed institutional changes is doubtful. Following the fall of Marcos in the Philippines, there was a major thrust towards a significant values shift and its institutionalization that is still not yet accomplished. Values cannot be imposed and, even once accepted in principle, their institutionalization takes time.

77 I learned of Parker Palmer's concept of a Movement Approach to Social Change after I had articulated my own thesis. The two approaches seem entirely congruent but with some difference in emphasis inasmuch as mine stresses the importance: first, of investing in conversations as the basis for supporting individuals in their personal work; second, of making explicit the underlying values aspirations that drive change; third, of directing conversations not solely to changes in personal behavior but also to

addressing institutional behavior. However, these seem to be matters only of explicit emphasis.

78 Hawken (2007)

79 The title of a UN Conference.

80 UNICEF has led the way in adopting a rights-based approach, focusing on the rights of the child. However, the rights of the child are inseparable from women's rights, the right to livelihood and other rights, and the agency-coordinated programming that this calls for has yet to be achieved.

81 UNDP (2002)

82 Sandel (1996)

83 I was a member of a committee of twelve charged with the revision of the book of *Faith and Practice* of the Pacific Yearly Meeting of the Religious Society of Friends (Quakers). These twelve people came with distinctively different backgrounds, perceptions, and vocabularies. Yet they were able to come to unity over the most fundamental expressions of faith and practice. Moreover, a preliminary edition of the revised version was circulated to the Yearly Meeting's 1,200 members and the committee responded to the hundreds of comments received from them coming to unity on their responses and with revisions that found unity among the members of the Yearly Meeting. (Pacific Yearly Meeting of the Religious Society of Friends (Quakers) *Faith and Practice,* 2001)

84 However, this is not to discount other practices that may educe collective wisdom. It is simply that this is one that I can speak of from experience.

85 "Centering" is the term more commonly used by Quakers rather than "grounding."

Bibliography

Ackerman, Peter and Jack Duvall, 2000. *A Force More Powerful* New York NY: Palgrave.

Anderson, Walter Truett, 1997. *The Future of the Self.* Los Angeles CA: Tarcher.

Armstrong, Karen, 2006. *The Great Transformation: The Beginning of Our Religious Traditions.* New York: Random House.

Atlee, Tom, 2003. *The Tao of Democracy: Using Co-Intelligence to Create a World That Works for All.* Cranston, RI: The Writers' Collective.

Austin, James, 1999. *Zen and the Brain.* Cambridge MA: MIT Press.

Bache, Christopher M., 2000. *Dark Night, Early Dawn.* Albany NY: SUNY Press.

Baum, Gregory, 1996. *Karl Polanyi on Ethics and Economics.* Montreal: McGill-Queen's University Press.

Beck, Don Edward & Christopher C. Cowan, 2005. *Spiral Dynamics.* Hoboken NJ: Wiley-Blackwell.

Beck, Don Edward and Christopher C. Cowan, 1996. *Spiral Dynamics: Mastering Values, Leadership, and Change.* Bodmin, Cornwall: MPG Books.

Beck, Don Edward and Graham Linscott, 1991. *The Crucible: Forging South Africa's Future.* Hawthorn, Australia: New Paradigm Press.

Bellah, Robert, 2007. *Habits of the Heart.* Berkeley CA: University of California Press.

Bellah, Robert, Richard Madsen, Steven M. Tipton, William M. Sullivan, and Ann Swidler, 1992 *The Good Society.* New York NY: Vintage.

Berlin, Isaiah, 1991. *The Crooked Timber of Humanity: Chapters in the History of Ideas.* Henry Hardy, Ed. New York: Alfred A Knopf, New Edition.

Briskin, Alan, Sheryl Erickson, John Ott, and Tom Callanan, 2001. *Centered on the Edge: Mapping a Field of Collective Intelligence and Spiritual Wisdom.* Kalamazoo MI: Fetzer Institute.

Burke, James, 2007. *Connections.* New York NY: Simon and Schuster.

Capra, Fritjof, 1984. *The Turning Point: Science, Society, and the Rising Culture.* New York NY: Bantam.

Cox, Gray, 2005. Communal Discernment and Academic Research: Is there a Quaker Epistemology for the Study of Public Policy and Social Change? *Friends Association for Higher Education Conference* <quakerinstitute.org/?page_id=69>.

Csikszentmihaly, Mihaly, 1993. *The Evolving Self.* New York: Harper Collins Publishers.

Damasio, Antonio R., 1999. *The Feeling of What Happens: Body and Emotion in the Making of Consciousness. New York NY: Harcourt Brace.*

Diamond. Jared, 2005. *Germs, Guns, and Steel.* New York NY: W.W. Norton.

Diamond, Jared, 2005. *Collapse: How Societies Choose to Fail or Succeed,* New York: Penguin Group.

Elgin, Duane, 1993. *Awakening Earth: Exploring the Evolution of Human Culture and Consciousness.* New York NY: William Morrow & Co.

Falk, Richard, 2000. *Human Rights Horizons.* London: Routledge.

Fowler, James W., 1981. *Stages of Faith: The Psychology of Human Development and the Quest for Meaning.* San Francisco: Harper.

Gellner, Ernst, 1992. *Postmodernism, Reason and Religion.* New York: Routledge.

Gergen, Kenneth, 1992. *The Saturated Self: Dilemmas of Identity In Contemporary Life.* New York NY: Basic Books.

Goldstein, Joseph and Jack Kornfield, 2001. *Seeking the Heart of Wisdom: The Path of Insight Meditation.* Berkeley CA: Shambhala.

Goleman, Daniel, 2011. *The Brain and Emotional Intelligence: New Insights.* Northampton MA: More Than Sound.

Graves, James Bau, 2004. *Cultural Democracy: The Arts, Community, and the Public Purpose.* Champaign IL: University of Illinois Press.

Greenspan, Stanley I. and Beryl Lieff Benderly, 1997. *The Growth of the Mind: And the Endangered Origins of Intelligence,* Cambridge Massachusetts: Perseus Books.

Habermas, Jürgen, 1979. *Communication and the Evolution of Society.* Boston MA: Beacon Press.

Hall, Brian P., 2000. *The Genesis Effect.* Makati City: Don Bosco Press.

Hall, Brian P., 2006. *Values Shift,* 2nd ed. Eugene OR: Resource Publications.

Harman, Willis W. and Elisabet Sahtouris, 1998. *Biology Revisioned,* Berkeley CA: North Atlantic Books.

Hawken, Paul, 2007. *Blessed Unrest: How the Largest Movement in the World Came Into Being and Why No One Saw It Coming.* New York NY: Viking Penguin.

Hawken, Paul, Amory Lovins and L. Hunter Lovins, 2008. *Natural Capitalism: Creating the Next Industrial Revolution.* New York NY: Back Bay Books.

Heifetz, Ronald, 1998. *Leadership Without Easy Answers.* Cambridge, MA: Harvard University Press.

Helmuth, Keith, 2003. U.S. Exceptionalism vs. Human Solidarity. *Friends Journal* June 2005, p. 6.

Hock, Dee W., 2000. *The Birth of the Chaordic Age.* San Francisco CA: Berrett-Koehler Publishers.

Hubbard, Barbara Marx, Barry Weins and Wabun Wind,1993. *The Evolutionary Journey: A Personal Guide to a Positive Future*

Huxley, Aldous, 1959. *The Human Situation: Lectures at Santa Barbara.* New York NY: HarperCollins Publishers.

Ignatieff, Michael, 2001. *The Needs of Strangers. New York NY*: Picador.

James, Sarah and Torbjorn Lahti, 2004. *The Natural Step for Communities: How Cities and Towns can Change to Sustainable Practices.* Vancouver, Canada: New Society Publishers.

Korten, David C., 2005. *The Great Turning: From Empire to Earth Community.* San Fransisco: Berrett-Kohler Publishers, Inc.

Lakoff, George, 2002. *Moral Politics: How Liberals and Conservatives Think.* Chicago: University of Chicago Press.

Lakoff, George and Mark Johnson, 1999. *Philosophy in the Flesh: The Embodied Mind and its Challenge to Western Thought.* New York NY: Basic Books.

Layard, P. R. G., 2005. *Happiness: Lessons from a New Science.* New York: Penguin Group.

Lietaer, Bernard, 2002. *The Future of Money.* New York NY: Random House.

MacIntyre, Alasdair, 2007. *After Virtue: A Study in Moral Theory,* Third Ed. Notre Dame: University of Notre Dame Press.

Maturana, Humberto R. and Francisco J. Varela, 1998. *The Tree of Knowledge: The Biological Roots of Human Understanding,* Boston MA: Shambhala.

McKibben, Bill, 2006. *The End of Nature.* New York NY: Random House.

Miller, William R. & Janet C'de Baca, 2001. *Quantum Change: When Epiphanies and Sudden Insights Transform Ordinary Lives.* New York NY: The Guilford Press.

Nagler, Michael N., 2003. *Is There No Other Way? The Search for a Nonviolent Future.* San Francisco CA: Inner Ocean Publishing.

Polanyi, Karl, 2001. *The Great Transformation: The Political and Economic Origins of Our Time.* Boston MA: Beacon Press.

Popper, Karl Raimond, 1964. *The Poverty of Historicism.* New York: Harper & Row.

Potter, Dave, John Ott, Cherrie Hafford, eds., 2001. *Centered on the Edge.* Chatanooga: Fetzer Institute.

Rand, Ayn, 1952 *The Fountainhead.* New York: Penguin Putnam.

Ray, Paul H., 2002. The New Political Compass. *Yes!* 7:3.

Ray, Paul H. and Sherry Ruth Anderson, 2001. *The Cultural Creatives: How 50 Million People Are Changing the World.* New York NY: Three Rivers Press.

Sandel, Michael J., 1996. America's Search for a New Public Philosophy, *Atlantic Monthly,* March.

Sandel, Michael J., 1998. *Democracy's Discontents: America in Search of a Public Philosophy.* Boston MA: Belknap Press.

Scheff, Thomas J., 2000. *Bloody Revenge: Emotions, Nationalism and War.* Bloomington IN: iUniverse.

Sheeran, Michael J., S.J., 1983. *Beyond Majority Rule: Voteless Decisions in the Religious Society of Friends.* Philadelphia: Philadelphia Yearly Meeting of the Religious Society of Friends.

Sen, Amartya, 1999. *Development as Freedom.* New York NY: Anchor Books.

Taylor, Charles, 1989. *Sources of the Self: The Making of the Modern Identity.* Cambridge, MA: Harvard University Press.

Turnbull, Colin M., 1972. *The Mountain People,* New York NY: Simon & Schuster.

United Nations Development Programme, 2002. *Development Policy Journal: Capacity for Sustainable Development.*

Varela, Francisco J., Evan T. Thompson and Eleanor Rosch, 1992. *The Embodied Mind: Cognitive Science and Human Experience.* Cambridge MA: MIT Press.

Vaughan, Frances, 2001. *The Inward Arc: Healing in Psychotherapy and Spirituality.* Bloomington IN: iUniverse.

Walsh, Roger, 1993. *Paths Beyond Ego.* Los Angeles CA: Tarcher.

Wilber, Ken, 1995. *Sex, Equality, Spirituality,* Boston MA: Shambhala.

Wilber, Ken, 2000. *Integral Psychology: Consciousness, Spirit, Psychology, Therapy.* Boston MA: Shambhala.

Wright, Robert, 2001. Nonzero: *The Logic of Human Destiny.* New York NY: Vintage.

Yergen, Daniel, and Joseph Stanislaw, 2002. *The Commanding Heights: The Battle for the World Economy.* New York NY: Free Press.

Hall-Tonna Values Map:
Short Values Definitions

Phase I *Surviving*

1 Safety—Goals

Self Interest/Control: Exercising personal control and, if necessary, control over others.

Self Preservation: Watching the bottom line and protecting one's self from financial or physical disaster.

Wonder/Awe/Fate: Appreciating and feeling helpless in the face of the grandeur and mystery of life.

1 Means of Attaining Goals

Food/Warmth/Shelter: Making sure that basic needs for board and lodging are met.

Function/Physical: Being concerned about the ability to care for oneself.

Safety/Survival: Having concern about health, safety and having enough to minimally sustain life.

2 Security—Goals

Physical Delight: Positively experiencing the senses and the body as a whole.

Security: Creating an environment where one feels one's most basic needs are met, such as health-care benefits or salary.

2 Means of Attaining Goals

Affection/Physical: Expressing fondness by touching.

Economics/Profit: Establishing financial stability.

Property/Control: Developing skills in managing property and finances.

Sensory Pleasure/Sexuality: Recognizing and appreciating the physical, emotional and psychological differences between genders.

Territory/Security: Defending and maintaining property.

Wonder/Curiosity: Desiring to explore nature with a sense of marvel and amazement.

Phase II *Belonging*

3 Family—Goals

Family/Belonging: Nurturing close and loyal relationships with one's family and/or co-workers.

Fantasy/Play: Engaging in imaginative activities for amusement or brainstorming new ideas.

Self Worth: Knowing that those who know one well value one.

3 Means of Attaining Goals

Being Liked: Experiencing affirmation by peers.

Care/Nurture: Consciously supporting family, friends and work-mates, and being emotionally supported by them.

Control/Order/Discipline: Being disciplined and orderly according to established rules no matter how stressful the circumstances are.

Courtesy/Hospitality: Being treated and treating others politely with respect.

Dexterity/Coordination: Skills in physical and mental coordination.

Endurance/Patience: Handling difficult and painful tasks with calm and perseverance.

Equilibrium: Maintaining status quo by managing conflicts.

Friendship/Belonging: Being part of a group with whom one can share day-to-day.

Obedience/Duty: Complying with established moral and legal obligations of management.

Prestige/Image: Appearing successful to gain the esteem of others.

Rights/Respect: Recognizing the worth, accomplishments and property of others.

Social Affirmation: Receiving support, affirmation and respect from peers.

Support/Peer: Giving and receiving support from one's peers even in difficult times.

Tradition: Recognizing and celebrating personal, cultural, organizational and national history.

4 Institution—Goals

Belief/Philosophy: Adherence to a belief system, set of principles, or established philosophy of life.

Competence/Confidence: Having assurance in one's skills to achieve and make a positive contribution at work.

Play/Recreation: Placing a priority on playful relaxation as essential to the quality of relationships and work.

Work/Wealth/Value: Providing for self and family.

4 Means of Attaining Goals

Achievement/Success: Driven to complete projects and accomplish something noteworthy.

Administration/Control: Exercising given authority to complete specific management tasks.

Communication/Information: Transmitting ideas and factual data between people and components of an organization.

Competition: Being energized to win and do better for one's self and as part of a team.

Design/Pattern/Order: Applying creative design through art, ideas or technology.

Duty/Obligation: Loyalty to managers, peers and the organization's customs and regulations.

Economics/Success: Managing financial resources to attain prosperous results.

Education/Certification: Completing a formal learning program.

Efficiency/Planning: Making critical path planning that maximizes output and minimizes waste.

Hierarchy/Order: Being able to understand and manage bureaucracy.

Honor: Promoting respect and loyalty to people in authority.

Short Values Definitions *(cont'd)*

Law/Rule: Living by the rules established by the legal system.

Loyalty/Fidelity: Duty to friends and to those in authority even when it is to your disadvantage.

Management: Coping with one's affairs by giving guidance to family or employees in accordance with one's philosophy and beliefs and the goals of the institution.

Membership/Institution: Taking pride in belonging to and working in the organization.

Ownership: Taking pride in what you own and the responsibilities you have.

Patriotism/Esteem: taking pride in one's country, its unique culture and its products.

Productivity: Being energized by completing and achieving personal and group tasks and goals.

Reason: Thinking logically and exercising reason before emotions.

Responsibility: Being accountable and in charge of a specific area or project.

Rule/Accountability: Behaving according to established codes of conduct.

Technology/Science: Applying scientific methods to create new inventions and tools.

Unity/Uniformity: Achieving efficiency, order, loyalty, and conformity to established norms in an organization.

Workmanship/Art/Craft: Producing artifacts or products that modify or beautify the person-made environment.

Phase III *Self-Initiating*

5 Vocation—Goals

Equality/Liberation: Recognizing that one has the same value and rights as others.

Integration/Wholeness: Harmonizing the mind and body.

Self Actualization: Developing spiritual, psychological, physical and mental health.

Service/Vocation: Knowing that you have skills, occupation, or profession that is making a significant contribution.

5 Means of Attaining Goals

Adaptability/Flexibility: Adjusting readily to changing conditions.

Authority/Honesty: Exercise of personal power as the straightforward expression of feelings and thoughts.

Congruence: Ability to express feelings and thoughts consistent with internal experiences in a straightforward manner.

Decision/Initiation: Starting projects and a course of action based on personal conviction, without getting other's approval.

Empathy: Listening and responding to others so they see themselves with more clarity, seeing and feeling their concerns and issues as they do.

Equity/Rights: Ensuring that all employees and peers are treated fairly.

Expressiveness/Joy: Sharing one's vision of the future, feelings and ideas openly and spontaneously so others are free to do the same.

Generosity/Compassion: Being sensitive to the limitations of others and using one's unique gifts and skills to help them without expecting something in return.

Health/Healing: Engaging in ongoing preventive health practices that are sound, such as diet, exercise and relaxation.

Independence: Thinking and acting for oneself without being constrained by external authority.

Law/Rule: Living by the rules established by the legal system.

Limitation/Acceptance: Recognizing personal inabilities as a beginning point for problem solving and growth.

Mutual Obedience: Being equally responsible for establishing a group's rules and following them.

Quality/Evaluation: Appreciating objective self-appraisal. Being open to what others reflect about oneself or one's group and the products of one's work for personal growth and the improvement of service to others.

Relaxation: Engaging in diversion from physical or mental work in order to reduce stress so that one's potential can be realized.

Search/Meaning/Hope: Seeking to discover one's uniqueness and to make sense out of day-to-day existence.

Self Assertion: Communicating one's thoughts and feelings and the value of one's point of view.

Sharing/Listening/Trust: Hearing another person's thoughts and feelings and expressing one's own in a climate of mutual confidence.

6 New Order—Goals

Art/Beauty: Experiencing intense pleasure through the inherent value of natural and person-made creations.

Being Self: Acting interdependently from the awareness of personal limitations, skills and know-how.

Construction/New Order: Developing the organization and its mission or a new organizational structure.

Contemplation: Practicing the art of meditation in order to achieve quality presence.

Faith/Risk/Vision: Willingness to risk and commit to a vision, mission, or plan of action based on one's values.

Human Dignity: Promoting an organizational environment where all people are respected and have their basic needs met so they can develop their full potential.

Knowledge/Insight: Pursuing truth through patterned investigation and use of intuition as a basis for decision-making.

Presence: Being attentive to others in a high quality way, so their lives become more meaningful.

6 Means of Attaining Goals

Accountability/Ethics: To act on personal moral principles even when faced with pressure to do otherwise.

Collaboration: Cooperating interdependently with personnel at all levels through appropriately delegating responsibility.

Community/Supportive: Creating cooperative groups of peers that provide mutual support to enhance quality of work and human interaction based on common values.

Complementarity: Enabling people to work together so their unique skills supplement, support and enhance each other.

Corporation/New Order: To be energized by creating and improving the organization, its quality and management efficiency.

Creativity: Sharing and applying new and original ideas and thoughts.

Detachment/Solitude: The regular discipline of detachment that leads to quality relationships with others.

Discernment: Enabling group consensus through openness, reflection, and honest interaction.

Education/Knowledge: Loving learning for its own sake and seeking comprehensive information from a variety of sources in order to make informed decisions.

Growth/Expansion: Enabling the organization to develop appropriate growth strategies.

Intimacy: Sharing thoughts, feelings and fantasies, mutually, freely, and regularly with another person.

Justice/Social Order: Acting to address, confront and correct conditions of human oppression.

Leisure: Engaging in highly skilled activities that totally detach you from the stress of work and increase your overall creativity.

Limitation/Celebration: Celebrating limitations as a way of defining unique skills and abilities.

Mission/Objectives: Managing of the strategic planning of an organization.

Mutual Accountability: Maintaining a reciprocal balance of tasks and assignments with others so that all are answerable for their own areas of responsibilities.

Pioneerism/Innovation: Giving leadership through pioneering new creative ideas.

Research: Patterning investigation in order to create new practical insights and/or technology that improve the quality of life.

Ritual Communication: Increasing human awareness and consciousness using

Short Values Definitions (cont'd)

ceremony, media, technology and the arts.

Simplicity/Play: Seeing simplicity in complexity as a basis for decision-making, leadership and lifestyle.

Unity/Uniformity: Achieving efficiency, order, loyalty, and conformity to established norms in an organization.

Phase IV *Inter-Dependent* Goals

7 Wisdom—Goals

Intimacy/Solitude: Experiencing inner harmony that results from meditation, mutual openness and acceptance of another person.

Truth/Wisdom: Reflecting on complex data to develop integrated and practical insights about the interrelationships of people and systems.

7 Means of Attaining Goals

Community/Personalist: Committing to a group or team to maximize both independent creativity and interdependent cooperation.

Interdependence: Giving preference to cooperation, both personal and inter-organizational, over independent action.

Minessence: Taking complex ideas from different sources and converting them into simplified, practical technology that improves society.

Prophet/Vision: Developing the ability to raise the awareness and activities of others to the subject of global human issues.

Synergy: Energizing group relationships so as to maximize the creation of new ideas and projects.

Transcendence/Solitude: Exercising spiritual discipline that enhances a global and visionary perspective.

8 World Order—Goals

Ecology/Global: aspiration to take authority for the created order of the world and to enhance its beauty and balance through creative technology in ways that have worldwide influence.

Global Harmony: Promoting quality of life internationally by influencing positive change relative to equality, conflict resolution and ecology.

Word: Transforming other people's values and worldviews through communicating of universal truths.

8 Means of Attaining Goals

Convivial Technology: Developing usable practical technology to improve the quality of life.

Global Justice: Bringing about inter-institutional interaction to provide the basic rights and necessities for the disadvantaged.

Human Rights: Committing one's resources to assure basic global human rights.

Macroeconomics: Managing financial resources within and between institutions to enhance stability and the quality of life for people.

83

Author Biography

Leonard Joy was an economist in academia for 30 years. He held posts at Makerere University College of East Africa, London School of Economics, Cambridge University, Institute of Development Studies at the University of Sussex, and University of California at Berkeley.

He has consulted for the World Bank and other United Nations agencies (FAO, WHO, UNICEF, UNESCO, IFAD, UNDP, ADB, and UNHCHR) as well as USAID, the UK Ministry for Overseas Development, and the Ford and Rockefeller Foundations. He contributed to the development of policy papers, operations manuals, and training programmes (including workshops on governance capacity development, for both high-level government and UNDP officials). Under UNDP auspices, he has had retainer contracts with several governments as a process consultant supporting efforts at governance systems change and systemic governance capacity development.

He is becoming increasingly focused on the understanding of values development and the application of this understanding, especially with regard to the need for values shifts in response to global climate change. He has a book in process tentatively entitled *Our Values Will Determine Our Future*.

As a Quaker, he is especially interested in the wider relevance of Quaker process and organization. He was a member of the committee for the revision of the book of Faith and Practice of the Pacific Yearly Meeting of the Religious Society of Friends. He served as Clerk of the Peace and Social Order Committee of Pacific Yearly Meeting concerned for Quaker corporate witness. He was the founding Clerk of a Quaker "think tank"—the Quaker Institute for the Future in 2003 and served in that capacity for seven years.

Quaker Institute for the Future
Advancing a global future of inclusion, social justice, and ecological integrity through participatory research and discernment.

The Quaker Institute for the Future (QIF) seeks to generate systematic insight, knowledge, and wisdom that can inform public policy and enable us to treat all humans, all communities of life, and the whole Earth as manifestations of the Divine. QIF creates the opportunity for Quaker scholars and practitioners to apply the social and ecological intelligence of their disciplines within the context of Friends' testimonies and the Quaker traditions of truth seeking and public service.

The focus of the Institute's concerns include:

- Economic behavior that increasingly undermines the ecological processes on which life depends.

- The development of technologies and capabilities that hold us responsible for the future of humanity and the Earth.

- Structural violence and lethal conflict arising from the pressures of change, increasing inequity, concentrations of power and wealth, declining natural capital, and increasing militarism.

- The increasing separation of people into areas of poverty and wealth, and into social domains of aggrandizement and deprivation.

- The philosophy of individualism and its socially corrosive promotion as the principal means for the achievement of the common good.

- The complexity of global interdependence and its demands on governance systems and citizen's responsibilities.

- The convergence of ecological and economic breakdown into societal disintegration.

<quakerinstitute.org>